The Courtship Dance
of the Borderline

The Courtship Dance of the Borderline

ANTHONY WALKER, MD

Writer's Showcase
San Jose New York Lincoln Shanghai

The Courtship Dance of the Borderline

Writer's Showcase
an imprint of iUniverse.com, Inc.

For information address:
iUniverse.com, Inc.
5220 S 16th, Ste. 200
Lincoln, NE 68512
www.iuniverse.com

ISBN: 0-595-19712-4

Printed in the United States of America

FOREWORD

The Courtship Dance Of The Borderline

The author's personal account of his involvement with someone having borderline personality disorder is lurid, frightening, fascinating, and compelling. Though more sexy that most such involvements, this account realistically captures the characteristically intense appeals and disillusionments that can be expected. The author's training as a doctor and psychiatrist uniquely qualify him to balance the highly emotionally recounting of his personal experiences with the clinically detailed record of events and circumstances. The borderline person's—in this case, the author's former wife, Jacqueline—remarkable capacity to transform apparent self-confidence, charm, and promise into helplessness, rage, or suicidal urges are vividly brought to life. It's clear that the author only had the perspective necessary to write this lucid account many years later, after first having gained the needed distance and perspective to enable him to recommit himself to his work, refind his bearings, and launch a new life.

But what of Jacqueline's family? Though the author recognized that Jacqueline's family had the same sense of unwanted responsibility as himself, he also poignantly noted that they did not have the same option of leaving. He, as a husband, together with the parents had offered a "holding environment" that was helpful to Jacqueline. Still, his usually generous compassion was restrained when he came to them, insofar as it was hard for him not to hold them responsible for causing Jacqueline's problems. The sorry truth is that with respect to borderline personality disorder, there are rarely villains. Borderline personality disorder probably doesn't come into full bloom without the nourishment provided by families, but the potential to become borderline is inborn and the nourishment provided by families is almost always unwitting. It's just that the world of someone with borderline personality disorder is always filled with heroes and villains, and if you're not one you're the other.

This book is an important statement that will enhance public consciousness about a disorder that is universally recognized and widely discussed within mental health circles. Borderline personality disorder has levels of prevalence, social dysfunction, health care utilization, and chronicity that make its public health significance similar to that of other major psychiatric disorders such as schizophrenia, bipolar disorder, or major depression, yet it has not received comparable attention. Why is this? The answer can be found in this book. Borderline personality disorder often leaves those who become intimately involved feeling guilty, helpless, and like they have personally failed. This is most true for family members or spouses, but it is also true for most clinicians. These are hardly the experiences that people want to "go public" with.

As much as I embrace the hope that this book will increase public consciousness about a neglected psychiatric disorder, I also have hopes that it will find a place within the training of mental health clinicians. Such trainees are typically overworked, but this book will certainly keep their attention. Alongside the movie, "Fatal Attraction," the book and movie "Girl Interrupted," and the psycho-biographical accounts of the borderline personality found in books about Princess Diana and Marilyn

Munroe, this book can titillate even as it teaches. Amongst this book's take home messages for clinicians is the value, if not the necessity, of working with others in order to keep one's perspective. Even more important is the message that the borderline patients' significant others—notably parents or spouses—experience the same dilemmas as clinicians without having the same sources of support. They need to be recruited as allies in treatment, just as this book's author has become.

John G. Gunderson, M.D.
McLean Hospital

July 2001

ACKNOWLEDGEMENTS

On reading a draft of this book, a very dear friend of mine remarked as to how unrelenting the book was. She said that she felt despair as the story progressed, and wondered if I couldn't describe what else had happened besides my intense and pathological relationship with Jacqueline. I thought about this for a while and realized that I couldn't come up with any such anecdotes. The truth is that this relationship permeated every aspect of my being and my experience. I made every choice in the context of what Jacqueline would think, feel, act or react. I couldn't ever totally relax, not until the very end. The relationship was unrelenting in its demands on my being. It is hard to write that without it sounding self-piteous, but that's what it was.

I have a few thank-yous. Firstly, to Bill Malamud, a kind and thoughtful psychiatrist and supervisor, who offered me the title for the book. Then to my family, who stuck with me throughout the ordeal. To Tim, Aaron, Jan, Angelo, Hans, Howard, Gary, Jerry and Charmaine for still being there at the end. To Penny and Alice, who found each misplaced comma. But I could never have done this without Lauren. More than anyone, she first helped me heal, and then patiently and objectively read every word many times until it made some kind of sense.

And ultimately to Dr John Gunderson, who gave me the final encouraging push.

CHAPTER I

August 1984
Johannesburg General Hospital
Johannesburg, South Africa

I was late to rounds that morning. Already the group had moved on from the first patient, so I snuck in quietly with the other students at the back of the group. In the pecking order of medical school, we stood behind the interns, who stood behind the residents, who stood behind the professor. My cover was secure.

"Jacqueline W. is a 22-year-old single white female who was admitted from the ER last night where she had presented in an unconscious state after she overdosed on amitryptiline." I pulled out my pocket drug-reference book and discovered that amitryptiline was in a class of anti-depressant medications that led to serious heart complications and even death when a patient overdoses. "First we pumped her stomach." I noticed a large plastic tube in her nose. The tube was draining into a bag at the side of her bed. "And then we gave her charcoal." This absorbed any remaining drug in her gut, according to my book. "Although her blood level was above the normal range, we monitored her heart rate and rhythm through the night and she appears to be doing well," continued the resident.

The crowd moved on to the next patient, giving me an opportunity to have a closer look at our suicide attempt. Her lips were still black from the charcoal that she had been forced to drink. Her nose was bent and swollen from the pull of the naso-gastric tube leading to the half-filled bag of stomach contents. Not a pretty sight. She did have nice eyes, though. "Why did she do it?" I wondered, staring at the young woman.

"...and Mr. Walker, can you give us a differential diagnosis for an elderly patient with an enlarged liver?" We had moved on to the next patient. I was still staring and wondering.

Our work on the unit took the rest of the morning, and the afternoon was filled with lectures, but my thoughts were stuck on the young woman. "Why would anyone so young want to take her life?" I thought to myself. I needed to know because it made no sense.

Later that day, the senior resident caught up with me. "You're interested in psych, aren't you? I want you to present a case on Monday. The chief of psychiatry is doing rounds on Monday, so I want you to pick a case with a psychiatric component."

"I'm going to interview that amitryptiline overdose," I told my class-mate, Howard.
"She's cute," he laughed, "but remember, she's one of ours, you know, the Chosen People!"

Howard was my sidekick and mentor that year, our final one of medical school. An Orthodox Jew, he refused to let me drive him to the hospital on Saturdays for morning rounds. I would wind up following him in my car as he walked briskly up the road leading to the medical school, all the time arguing action versus intention. "Just get in the car," I would insist, "it's not out of my way!" But he would persist in his walking, telling me that he didn't expect a shaygetz like me to understand. We hardly ever talked medicine; instead we spent hours exploring "The Human Mind" as if only we knew the secrets to its inner workings and reason. Like me, he had decided to go to medical school in order to study psychiatry. I wanted to work with children, and he wanted to help adults, and together we planned to fix mankind's problems. "You know, Howard, I'm going to specialize in child psychiatry. I'll find a way to cure kids of all their worries. That way you won't have a job when I'm done," I would tease him.

"After they're finished with you, they'll all need my help," would be his retort.

The next morning I was early to rounds, but that did not change the hierarchy and I stood at the back with my group. When we got to her bed, I peered over Howard's shoulder to get a closer look. Later she would tell me that she had noticed me staring. "God, with your big nose and curly orange hair, I thought, 'Oy, a nice Jewish boy.'" The nose is Roman from Spanish ancestry. The curly orange hair was the unfortunate consequence of having used my housemate's shampoo. She had added a large quantity of peroxide to it to maintain her blonde hair.

After rounds, I stopped in Jacqueline's room. The tubes and cables and monitors had been removed. Her dark hair was pulled back tight. Her large brown eyes filled a pretty face. Thin manicured eyebrows and high cheekbones framed her eyes. Soft cheeks tapered down to a dimpled chin. And then she smiled. It was a smile that stopped me from thinking what I was thinking. It stopped me from the purpose of my visit and instead left me gawking. Her face seemed so familiar, like that of a friend, but I couldn't place her. I continued to stare, and then I remembered. She was

Vivien Leigh. I had seen *Gone With the Wind* twice. There is a scene during the charity ball when Scarlett O'Hara is considering a second dance with Rhett Butler:

> *Rhett: Don't start flirting with me. I'm not one of your*
> *plantation beaus. I want more than flirting from you.*
> *Scarlett: What do you want?*
> *Rhett: I'll tell you, Scarlett O'Hara, if you'll take that*
> *Southern-belle simper off your face. Someday, I*
> *want you to say to me the words I heard you say*
> *to Ashley Wilkes: I love you!*

I fell in love with Jacqueline the moment she smiled. It was as simple as that.

"My name is Anthony. I am a final year medical student. I'd like to know more about you—I mean, talk to you so that I can present your case on Monday morning to the professor." She continued to smile, her head half cocked, as I struggled through my attempt to take a history. "What is your name? How old are you? Where do you live? What brought you in to the hospital?…I have to leave now. Maybe I can come back and finish tomorrow?"

"Sure," she smiled. Her smile was her weapon, her hook, and her magnet. I was mesmerized by it. The courtship dance had begun.

CHAPTER 2

Ashley: Isn't it enough that you've gathered every other man's heart today? You've always had mine. You cut your teeth on it.

Scarlett: Don't tease me now. Have I your heart my darling? I love you. I love you.

Ashley: You mustn't say such things. You'll hate me for hearing them.

Scarlett: I could never hate you. And I know you must care about me. Oh, you do care, don't you?

Ashley: Yes, I do care. Oh, can't we go away and forget we ever said these things?

Then later in the scene, she slaps Ashley:

I'll hate you till I die. I can't think of anything bad enough to call you.

I did not sleep well that night. In my dreams I visited Tara. Ironically, Johannesburg's most famous psychiatric hospital shared the same name, and only a few months earlier I had spent two weeks studying there on rotation.

I was anxious for the night to pass quickly so that I could get back to the hospital. My thoughts were filled with all the questions I would ask her. The next morning, a Saturday, I was up at 5:30. With the end of six years of medical school only three months away, the parties heralding graduation had begun. My friends and colleagues were preparing for these as much as they were preparing for the final exams, but I had some important business to attend to. I grabbed my white coat, stuffed a bagel in my mouth, and headed off. The nurses were surprised to see me on the ward.

"It's your day off! What are you doing here? Are you going to the party tonight?"

"I have to present a case on Monday. I came in to prepare."

I went into her room, where she was sitting comfortably in bed. Next to her was a large box of chocolates, mainly full of opened wrappers. She smiled, but this time I was prepared. "Good morning!" She took out a round chocolate and placed it slowly in her mouth, then seductively licked the tips of her fingers.

"So, where do we start?" she asked.

At medical school we are taught exactly what questions to ask. Although this is important, I was finding that it was not so much the question itself, as how the question is asked that brings the art of medicine to life. I tried hard not to appear nervous.

"What brought you to the hospital?"

"I took an overdose of pills."

"Can you tell me what happened?" I sat forward.

"I've been dating this guy, you see. He is rich, wonderful, and Jewish. Two months ago I found out that I was pregnant. Neither of us wanted the baby so I had an abortion. After that he stopped spending time with me. All he wanted to do was spend time with his friends, going to clubs and bars. He told me that it was too intense, that I was suffocating him. He told me that he needed space."

"Go on."

"I can't stand being alone. Men have always left me. They fall in love with me and then they leave me. Obviously I'm not good enough."

"What happened next?"

"I took a big piece of very delicious chocolate cake—you can see I looove chocolate—and I took a bottle of my mother's pills, and then I went to bed. My mother told me that she was going to go out for the day."

"How did they find you?"

"My mother called the house and the cleaning lady answered. She told the lady that she had something to tell me. The lady told her that she couldn't wake me up. I guess she called 911."

"Did you think you would die?"

"I did then, but I feel so good now, so good to be alive. I'm glad that I didn't die. But you know, this morning his mother called me and told me that I was a nice girl but that I couldn't see her son any more, and that I was not to try to contact him again. He's so fucking weak. He sends his mother to do a man's job. He's so insignificant. What did I ever see in him?"

She turned to look out of the hospital window, then bowed her head and started to cry, softly. I gave her a box of tissues and took her hand.

"It's going to be alright," I said, squeezing her hand. "Here, have another chocolate." She smiled.

I continued the interview. She was the oldest of four children. She had majored in art at college, and she loved to paint flowers. She told me that she would take a large canvas and draw bubbles upon bubbles of color in oil using big strokes until the whole thing fused into a field of flowers. One brother was a junior in college, majoring in math. He had a predilection for hanging out at casinos counting cards at blackjack and coming home at all hours, but he made money at it so her parents did not care. The youngest were identical twins, seniors in high school. Her parents were well-to-do and had a grand home in leafy suburbia.

She told me that her mother bullied her father around. Her mother was Jewish and her father Christian, so they celebrated both holidays. For her mother, the more holidays there were the better. She ran a cooking school and catering service that boomed during the holidays. "My dad doesn't confront my mother. He goes along with everything she says, but he can have a temper."

She loved her grandmother. "She has unconditional love for me, even when I need some extra money," laughed Jacqueline. "She's a real character. One day the telephone company came to her apartment saying that they had to fix her phone. She told them that it couldn't be because her phone wasn't broken, but that maybe it was the next-door phone. They knocked next door but the little old lady was out. She told them that they could use her balcony to get into the next-door apartment. Well, to cut a long story short, they went in through the balcony, robbed the neighbor and went out her front door. She even offered them a drink for the fine service that they were providing and for their inconvenience. But when her neighbor came home, oy, she never heard the last of it."

I still did not have a sense of why she had wanted to kill herself. She was so young, so vibrant, and so beautiful. My textbook taught that it was single, alcoholic, older men who were most at risk for committing suicide. She had told me that her life was not worth living after her boyfriend had left her, and that men had always left her. Why would anybody want to leave her? And even so, what could be so painful about being left that only death could relieve? I asked her more questions but had trouble focusing on her answers. She intrigued me in a way that I had never felt before. I felt myself staring at her face, examining it for some possible imperfection, but there was none. "I have no more questions. Thank you. Do you have any questions for me?"
"Yes, how old are you?"
"25. Why do you ask?"

"You are so young. You're the best doctor in the whole hospital," she laughed.

"Final year student," I corrected her as I floated out of the room. "I'll see you Monday."

The presentation was a disaster. Having concentrated only on the psychological aspects of the case, and suicide in general, I hadn't prepared any of the clinical material. My mind was not on the work. I felt embarrassed that I could not answer some of the more important aspects of tricyclic anti-depressant overdose. The chief of psychiatry saved the day by talking about the diagnosis and treatment of depression.

Despite the failure of my presentation, it was precisely because of my intrigue with the mind gone awry that I had gone to medical school. I wanted to study medicine to become a psychiatrist. I was fascinated that the most complex organ of all, the brain, often suffered the most, and yet there was nothing visibly broken that people could point to and understand. No one ever said "…and did you hear that Johnny had an accident and now he is serotonin-deficient and he is going to have to wear a cast on his head for the rest of his life?" It seemed that psychological pain was the least visible of all and the easiest to blame on the sufferer.

Afterwards, the chief pulled me aside. "Anthony, be careful. Don't get involved. She suffers from Borderline Personality Disorder. Read about it. She is very ill and very disturbed. I can see that you want to help her, but it is a very destructive disorder. She told you herself that men always ended up leaving her. It is so easy to miss because borderlines can be so charming and manipulative. She will need more and more from you, like a parasite, but you will never be able to give enough. She will suck you dry and destroy your spirit." I did not believe him. He was wrong. What Jacqueline needed was love. No one could charm and manipulate me. Anyway, he had warned me, so I would be on the lookout for manipulation. Moreover, she was going to be discharged that afternoon. It saddened me that she was leaving. I wanted to know more about her. Was she as kind as she was lovely? Did she now have dreams for the future? I wanted to know what it would feel like to hug her and tell her that I could take care of her. But I was happy that she looked as well as she did so soon after having made such a serious suicide attempt. I went into her room, "Goodbye."

"Goodbye," she said, extending her hand. I held it in mine, wondering how I could extend the time with her, but I had no ideas.

"Good luck. I'm sure that you'll be OK."

Howard was relieved. "Rescue fantasy, the classic pitfall of the novice therapist. I brought this paper for you that talks about it." It dealt with the finding that many inexperienced therapists feel that they can cure their borderline patients simply by trying as hard as they can and by caring enough. These novice therapists initially intrude into all aspects of their patient's life, causing the patient to increasingly depend on the therapist. For the therapist, there is great narcissistic appeal in being so needed, but there is also great disappointment as the work brings little change. Over time the therapist burns out, gradually growing to resent and blame the patient. Finally, the therapist can no longer meet what he feels to be the unrealistic demands of the patient, and terminates therapy. In the end the patient is hurt even further by this abandonment. "What a mess," I thought to myself. "Maybe it is true what some people say, that you have to be crazy to be a psychiatrist."

Howard's paper was interesting, but I failed to see what it had to do with me; that is to say, that his paper dealt concretely with patients and therapists. I had no intention of becoming her therapist. I wanted her to feel self-worth. I wanted to tell her that her life was not meaningless, that she had talents and grace, that she was funny and cute. Also I had no sense that this was a need to rescue her. She so quickly appeared happy and together that there didn't seem to be anything from which to rescue her. I reassured Howard that I could take care of myself.

That evening I went to the library. During our six years of medical school, we had only spent two weeks in the psychiatry wards. During that time, we learned about depression, mania and schizophrenia. No one mentioned personality disorders, so perhaps they weren't that important or pathological. Everyone I knew had an individual personality style. Some people were more difficult to deal with than others, but I didn't think that they had a "disorder." Howard had recommended a book by John Gunderson. "The guy is from McLean Hospital. It's the most famous psychiatric hospital in the world. He wrote a whole book on Borderline Personality*." I found the book, and noticed that it had only been checked out a handful of times. This reassured me that others didn't seem to worry too much about the condition. I read the chapter that described the criteria necessary to make the diagnosis of Borderline Personality Disorder, but other than the suicide attempt, Jacqueline didn't seem to meet any of the others. What struck me more than anything else was that she had been in such great spirits when she left the hospital after a one-day stay. The patients I had seen in the psychiatry wards remained there for weeks and months and looked depressed. Jacqueline didn't look like someone who had a long-term, severe psychiatric condition. I continued to read through Gunderson's book:

Although the concept of a transitional object seems more compatible with the observations on the dependency and separation sensitivity of Borderline patients than does the concept of a self-object, the distinction between these two concepts is murky.

I had spent only two weeks in psychiatry. I understood depression and that sometimes people heard voices that others could not hear, but the language of the book seemed very technical to me. What was a transitional object? What was separation sensitivity? How did these terms apply to Jacqueline? The book seemed so much more complicated than how she had presented. I doubted that she really had the disorder, but maybe I just didn't want to believe it.

* see Appendix 1

CHAPTER 3

My mother recently visited, regaling us with stories from my childhood. One day when I was nine years old, she took the family to the beach. A fisherman was casting his lines off the rocks nearby. I took my plastic pail and went to sit by him. Over the next hour, his catch was plentiful, but many fish were too small for his basket. He took them off the hook and threw them aside. Occasionally a brave gull would venture close to pick the easy meal. It saddened me that the fish might be suffering, so I filled my bucket with water and put the discarded fish into it before the gull or dry land could do them any further damage. Soon I had five fish and as the fisherman was done, I headed back to my family.

Once home, the fish did not appear to be all that happy as they swam sluggishly in the warm murky water. We had a small, plastic yard-pool, which we barely used but looked to be the right size for the fish. I filled the pool with fresh water and then dumped my bucket into it. Immediately the fish seemed to be in trouble. I hurried to tell my father, who explained that the fish would die because they were salt-water fish and couldn't live in fresh water. I ran to the kitchen and found the salt container, then headed back to the pool and dumped the entire salt load into the water. "Come on, fish, live. Come on fish," I pleaded, but to no avail.

She then told us of a time when I was a bit older and a neighbor came over with his new pellet gun. He aimed it at a pigeon sitting on a branch of a large oak in our yard and pulled the trigger. The bird dropped to the ground and started flopping about. I picked it up and saw that it had been shot through its left eye. Distressed, I took it to my mother and begged her to take me to the veterinarian so that we could save it. The bird died en route.

"You have always cared for the very weakest, the most hopeless cases," she observed, while making a pot of tea.

Perhaps that was why at medical school I had chosen to do an elective in a remote mountain village in rural South Africa. With few medical services and little education offered, prenatal care was rare in the village. One day, a young mother brought her three-week-old son into the clinic. He had been listless for two days. The mother's family didn't know of the child's existence. She was too ashamed to tell them, but now she was terrified of losing the child. She confessed that she had had a difficult time breastfeeding him. The child was terribly dehydrated, with sunken eyes and hollow belly. We couldn't even find a vein to give him fluids. Half an hour later the child died. That was the first time that I ever cried at medical school. It was also the last. An intern pulled me aside. "If it gets to you that bad each time they die, you gotta rethink this profession. It's going to happen all the time."

I cried not just for the death itself, but for how terrible it must have been for the mother, and the fears that had made her avoid seeking help. I cried for the loss and the guilt that she must have felt. I was angry that the apartheid system had failed this mother by not providing easy access to medical care. I promised myself that in the future I would not let my emotions affect my judgment, but I also promised myself not to lose sight of the need to take care of people.

CHAPTER 4

I kept thinking about Jacqueline during the week. I wondered how she was and what she was doing to take care of herself, but I resisted the urge to call her. On Thursday morning, the nurse manager handed me a message. Jacqueline's mother had called and wanted me to call back. She said it was important. My body tensed and my hands became clammy. I could hardly recall ever having felt as excited by anything before, especially something so seemingly insignificant. Yet it was the feeling of being fourteen and in love again, of waiting for the phone to ring after a first date.

"Hello, Mrs. W? This is Anthony. You had called looking for me? Is everything alright?"

"Oh, hello! I just wanted to tell you that Jacqueline is doing much better. We wanted to thank you for everything that you did."

"Really, I did nothing. You seem to have a nice family. You all pulled together when Jacqueline needed it most. It meant so much. It's that kind of love that heals."

"You don't understand. We haven't seen her this happy in a long time. Anyway, another reason I called is that a friend of ours is having a big party on Saturday. It is for their daughter who is turning twenty-one. Jacqueline was wondering if you would go as her escort. It would mean so much to her if you went. She doesn't have a date since she broke up with her boyfriend."

"I really don't see why not. I had been wondering how Jacqueline was doing. I'd be happy to go."

"Good! If you could, be here by seven for pre-party drinks." She gave me the directions to her house and I told her I'd be there on time. I wondered why Jacqueline herself had not called. Maybe if I had said "no," the rejection would have been too much after everything else that had happened. That evening I set out for my usual five-mile run. I noticed that I ran a little faster than usual, and then having completed the loop, I repeated the distance.

The rest of the week sped by until Saturday, when the clock seemed to stop. Every minute dragged on. I read the newspaper during breakfast, took a shower, and then shaved. But that only took up half an hour. I went for a long run, and then took another shower. I watched TV, then the clock. I tried to read to distract myself, but nothing helped. I could not keep Jacqueline out of my mind, and I thought of all the questions, still unanswered. Most puzzling was why she had tried to kill herself. She did not seem depressed. She was bright and engaging. Was it possible, as she had said, that she was so much in love with her boyfriend that breaking up was intolerable? But if so, why was she now so happy? Was it me? Had I made so much of an impression on her that our brief encounter let her believe that she could find such love again?

Eventually the time passed, and as evening approached I showered for the third time that day. I wore a pair of trendy olive-green jeans with black patent leather shoes and a light-blue, white-striped dress shirt. Unable to stop pacing, I left the house early and arrived at Jacqueline's with twenty minutes to spare. I drove around the block four or five times, not wanting to appear too eager. I parked the car outside the wrought-iron gates, which opened onto a long brick driveway. I blew air out forcibly through pursed lips, willing myself to relax, as I walked down to the house. As there was no doorbell I could find, I reached for the iron knocker, which was shaped in the form of a mermaid and had a welcoming smile. Jacqueline opened the door before I had a chance to knock.

Jacqueline glowed. She wore a low-cut floral dress, which she told me was Gianfranco. Her hair was pulled up, to open up her face, and then fell in soft braids onto her open back. Two large gold hoops dropped from soft lobes. Her white smile was made all the brighter by the contrast with her Revlon-red lips. Finally, high-heels helped to further define her well-toned and tanned legs. "Well, are you just going to stand there? Come and meet the rest of the family."

At the party she had assigned herself the role of designated drinker. She drank three glasses of a mediocre Merlot with dinner. "I don't usually drink this much," she laughed, "but I do feel less nervous when I drink." It was clear that I wasn't going to understand anything deep about her that night. It was not going to be a night for talking, so I joined her when a better Chardonnay was served. Eventually, the dance music started, and after each of the first three dances, she downed a glass of wine, but then abruptly stopped drinking. "I can't get too drunk tonight, you know. I've got plans."

She flirted conspicuously with admiring men, yet all the time stayed close to me. She reminded me of a child coyly playing peek-a-boo with strangers while holding on to her mother's leg. But there was more than just flirting and drinking. There was hip gyrating, jacket twirling and skirt hiking. There was laughing and teasing, playful taunting and hinting. We had been at the party for just over two hours, when she grabbed my hand and led me outside to where the cars were parked in neat rows. She pressed me back against my car. "Tonight you got the best and you know it. You saw the other men looking at me. You know they wanted me, but I am with you and I want you to take me home now."

I had never been on a date as unpredictable as this. I had been expecting a somewhat subdued evening spent in reflection and talk, but there had been little of either. Instead I was being seduced by a modern-day Scarlett O'Hara, and I was not inclined to stop the seduction. I opened the passenger door and she slid into her seat. It was difficult to concentrate on the drive, but it was even more difficult to believe that only a week earlier, modern medicine had ensured that her suicide attempt did not succeed. A tough, self-confident, sexiness had replaced vulnerability, innocence and openness. I tuned the radio to a local music station. She sang along with Tina Turner...

> You're simply the best, better than all the rest
> Better than anyone, anyone I've ever met
> I'm stuck on your heart, and hang on every word you say
> Tear us apart, baby I would rather be dead

I would caution any friend to be careful in a relationship with a potentially suicidal woman with few inhibitions, but the rational mind flooded by libido is no longer rational. This was a strange moment for me. I felt that I had been sucked into a new version of *Gone with the Wind*. I was the protagonist. Yet, I had lost sight of the fact that in Hollywood, the movies end after two hours. Moreover, after the show you get to go home. Even though the evening was unpredictable, it did not seem crazy. I could not tell how it would end and this uncertainty intrigued me. She was in total control now and this too was a new experience for me.

Her parents were still carousing with the hosts when we arrived at Jacqueline's house. "My parents won't be back for a while. You didn't have much to drink. My dad has a bottle of bubbly in the fridge. Let's toast to life!" she said handing me the bottle. I shook the champagne in the way racecar drivers do after having won a race, and the cork popped easily as the white foam spewed out. I found two flutes, and turned to offer her a drink. She had stripped down to her waist and held her breasts together in her cupped hands. "I want you to drink from me!" I nearly dropped the bottle and she laughed, "I want you to pour it between my breasts and drink from me. God that will turn me on!" The enchantment was complete, and I did as she instructed. As I poured and drank, she threw her head back and held my head to her chest. "Kiss my nipples," she insisted. Suddenly she pulled my head back. "Quick," she insisted, "Come with me to the living room!" I did not hear the car approaching. She stripped quickly and lay down on a plush white shag, directing me all the while with skilled hands. It was all the time I needed to reach a quick climax. She jumped up and quickly got dressed, urging me to do the same. Then she turned on the light. "Damn. Help me move this couch over the stain. I made a mess with my period. I'll clean it up tomorrow." We then sat on the couch as her parents entered the room. I felt awkward and disheveled. I sensed the sweat forming on my brow. She sat saintly cool.

"Hi dear. Have a nice time?"

"Yes, thanks mom. And Anthony took good care of me."

"Well, goodnight. Thanks for escorting Jacqueline." After a pause, she added, "Darling, please clean up the champagne before you go to bed. You spilled some on the floor in the kitchen."

CHAPTER 5

I drove home in an unsettled daze. There was a delicious impending sense of loss of control that appealed to every voyeuristic bone in my body. This was my own personal "Fatal Attraction." I had always enjoyed living on the edge, but on reflection my edges were safe and relatively sure; this was different. Now I had lost control with no certainty of safety. It was dangerously exhilarating, like a joy ride on a roller coaster in the dark after the park had closed for the day.

I was brought up in a devout Catholic family, the eldest of eight children. My mother lived by the belief that because we did not know either the time or the place of the Second Coming, any person could be the Messiah. We had to love and treat all people as if salvation itself depended on it. Her three sisters were nuns and there were great hopes that one of us would pursue a religious devotion. But despite the fish on Fridays, we laughed a lot. My mother regaled us with stories from our mischievous past. "Once I took Anthony to see my sister at the convent. While there we happened upon the Mother Superior. "Say 'Hello' to the Mother Superior," I told him. He was only four years old, and The Good Lord had not gifted her with any looks. He said, "Hello, Pig!" I told him to apologize immediately, and he was very ashamed and he hung his head and said 'Sorry, Pig.'"

The four oldest children were made the guardian angels of the four youngest. Our sacred task was to protect them from all dangers physical and spiritual. On this, too, salvation depended. Once my mother had entrusted my then six-year-old brother Michael to keep my fourteen-month-old sister Rachel entertained in her crib while my mother went upstairs to get a blanket for her. We were in the yard and the wind had picked up. As I was the oldest child, my mother told me to keep an eye on both of my siblings. She assured us that she would be right back. We had been collecting earthworms up until that point and we thought that showing them to my sister would entertain her. Immediately she started to cry, which Michael said meant that she was hungry. As salvation depended on caring for our younger siblings we fed her with the only thing at hand. Years later, National Geographic had an article about a farm in Minnesota that raised earthworms for their protein content and nutritional potential. Needless to say we did not have that article in our defense when my mother returned.

My father was a practical man, which is to say that things needed to make sense. There was little room in his worldview for "emotionalism" as he would call it. Emotions led to clouding of rational thought. Getting from A to B had to be in a straight line. If you wanted to pass a test you studied, and if you wanted to be number one in your class you studied hard. My mother, on the other hand, did not care as much about the test or our being number one, as long as we were happy. My father insisted that being number one would make us happy. He had little time for words not backed up by deeds.

He would be up at six in the morning and off to work, but then back by five to help with the homework. Each child had up to half an hour with him to review the homework. He would nurse a Scotch during the homework session but this did not dull his determination to see that every bit of schoolwork had been done. Fun for him was naming the capitals of obscure countries and it became a game that we played on Sundays during lunch. His serious manner made it a challenge for us to try to get him to ease up and laugh at silly things. Once Michael went to a farm fair and by an outrageous stroke of luck guessed the exact number of eggs in a huge container. The first prize was a one-month-old calf. When my mother picked us up, we loaded the calf into the back of the station wagon and drove the calf back to suburbia. We had a three-acre yard, so the calf would have plenty of grass to eat and room to roam. Moreover we had a middle-aged sheepdog that needed company, so the calf was a hit. Initially it spent time following the dog, which it regarded as its mother, it being the only other creature that ate on all fours. But soon it ranged more freely and visited the yards and gardens of our neighbors. The calf's need for food had increased dramatically and it was destroying increasingly larger patches of yard, although it deposited equivalent amounts of manure in return. It continued to grow and moved from soprano to tenor in a matter of weeks, mooing along with the dog at passing cars or pedestrians. One particularly hot summer day our bridge-playing neighbors came frantically to our house. They had left the gate to their pool open and our dog had jumped in. But of greater concern was that the bull had followed suit and could now not get out of the pool! The bull left the next day to an unknown destination, a place where, my father assured us, it would be well cared for. We boycotted beef for the next two months.

I recognized the differences between my home life and that of Jacqueline's. Although there were many moments of fun, pranks and outrageous adventure in our home, there was an underlying bedrock of faith and education in our home that was fundamental to the way that my parents had decided to structure our family. Jacqueline's family lived for the moment. Meaning came from the stimulation of the senses of smell, taste, feel, sight and hearing. Pleasure was an end in itself. This was a new and very appealing perspective for me.

Because of these differences, Jacqueline was not easily going to fit in. I worried that my parents would see her as godless and unmotivated in matters academic, hopeless enough to consider suicide and too cute to be anything but a distraction to a young man facing medical school finals. To me she was captivating and challenging. She had pain, sorrow and emptiness that only love and laughter would heal. She was the Messiah. My mother would understand.

CHAPTER 6

My parents seem to have decided on geographical diversity for the birthplace of their children. We were born in four countries on three continents; I in Indiana, my brother in England, four in Spain and two in South Africa. I have asked my father many times why we moved to South Africa, and his answer has changed as many times as I have asked him. When they lived in the United States, Kennedy had just been elected, and they moved to Europe about a year after his assassination. In Spain, Franco was slowly losing his grip on power, and in South Africa, we witnessed the transition to democracy from the Soweto uprisings to Mandela's release from prison. "Most people only read about what you guys have lived through," he often told us.

Nevertheless, South Africa, at least when we arrived there, was a highly conservative, puritanical society. Television was eventually introduced in 1976, but the only station was the state-run South African Broadcasting Corporation, and all we had to choose from was religious services, rugby or the government-sponsored news. The only illegal drug that was readily available was marijuana, which grew everywhere because of the ideal climate. I knew no one who had ever tried cocaine or heroin. X-rated and R-rated movies and magazines were non-existent. When somebody was able to sneak a *Playboy* through customs on return from an overseas trip, it was a grand coup. Citizenship was stratified between the races, and people of different groups could not legally live in each other's neighborhoods. News broadcasts were heavily censored, so internally we were barely aware of what was going on in our own country. Friends who had traveled overseas would return saying they had seen images of white policemen and soldiers shooting unarmed black Africans in the townships on the T.V. news in England, Australia and the United States. It was hard to believe that these stories were true.

All this matters because when we saw the portrayal of American life, as depicted in the few Hollywood movies that were allowed into South Africa, it seemed so much finer, so much more sophisticated, and so much more glamorous than the rigidity of South African life.

Perhaps it was naive to think that Hollywood life was real, but for us it was all that we had seen outside of our own world. Every South African's dream was to end up in America. So far my relationship with Jacqueline had the makings of a little slice of American life.

CHAPTER 7

Johannesburg
Late October 1984

For the next three months we were inseparable. At times it felt like more than that, almost as if we had merged into one being. "I cannot stand being away from you," she told me. "I can't stand that you go to the hospital and care for all those other people, that you are gentle with them and worry about how they do. I can't stand that you leave me every day to go to work. I want you to be with me for always and ever. Please don't ever leave me."

One evening we were walking through a downtown park. The evening was just beginning to cool down. We were sitting quietly on a bench beside a large old oak tree when the sprinklers suddenly came on. She jumped up in delight and skipped into the middle of the spray, drenching herself. The wet shirt outlined her body and it was evident that she was wearing nothing under the shirt. I laughed and followed her. She stopped dancing and started smiling, all the time slowly unbuttoning her shirt. She held my hands and pulled me down to the wet grass with her. I worried that we would be seen by passers-by, or worse, be arrested by the park police, but none of this seemed to matter to Jacqueline. She kissed me, and held my hands to her breasts. "Make love to me…"

To my detriment, I spent little time studying for final exams. Jacqueline was teaching me to eat oysters with a desire seldom associated with food. She would close her eyes and tease the oyster with her tongue while holding the shell tightly in her hands, all the while moaning softly. It was never vulgar. Her desperate need to feel was both seductive and intriguing. Eating was feeling, drinking was feeling, shouting was feeling, it was all about feeling deeply and genuinely. There were no pleasantries. If she did not like the awful food on her plate she sent it back, with little regard for the feelings of the waiter or the chef. "We paid for their food and for their service. We got neither. Fuck them. Next time they won't make the same mistake. If you don't demand the best, you'll never get it. We run around saying 'excuse me' and 'pardon me' when we mean 'give me the fucking service you promised!'" The honesty was so brutal and refreshing that it was hard to disagree. Being with her was being more alive than I had ever been. Each moment was unpredictable, provocative, talented, and exhilarating.

CHAPTER 8

I began to think seriously about my life with her, and how to make the future work. I had a job lined up, but she would need something to do to keep her busy during the long hours of my internship. Jacqueline had gone to art school to refine an evident talent. Her art was big and colorful, oils on canvas that filled beyond the frame. "I'll paint. I'll make you a beautiful home. I'll cook for you, and I'll love you. In return just never leave me. I have never felt such love from anybody. If you ever took it away from me I would die."

I knew that she had had boyfriends that she had cared about in the past, and I could not see why anybody would have wanted to leave her. "What happened to your first boyfriend?"

"I was thirteen and he was so wonderful. I remember that we were on vacation with my parents. I saw him lying by the pool with his friends. I went straight up to him and told him I wanted a drink. He was twenty, but I told him I was sixteen so that he wouldn't get into trouble. That night was my first time ever. We were together for five years, but then he joined the Airforce. He told me that he would spend every free moment with me. One day he told me to meet him at his apartment, but he was late. He knew not to piss me off, so I broke in. I waited and waited. I got so angry. God, I thought that he was with someone else, and the more I thought about it the angrier I became. I searched his whole apartment. I found a pile of old letters from his ex. I put them in the middle of his room on the rug and burnt them. It felt so good, you just don't know. How could he still keep them when he was with me? When he got back, he had some roses and chocolate for me. He found the mess, and after that he never trusted me again. He left me, like men always have. No, maybe I left him. I do that to weak men. Weak men have no balls. I need a man with balls and you have balls."

Jacqueline told me that she needed people who loved her. Once, when she was eighteen, she met a man, an actor, who instantly fell in love with her. He begged her to tour the country with him. He insisted that she would inspire him in his aspiring role as Macbeth. She agreed to go, and left without telling friends or family. "I think that my mom knew where I was, but she was happy to get rid of me for a while." She set off with the actor on his quest for stardom, but the demands of auditioning, and the frustrations of rejection made him too moody. "Sometimes he would get pissed at not having been given the part and he would go out drinking and not come home all night. It terrified me to be left alone in an apartment in a strange city. One morning, I called my mother. She wired me money and I left before he came home that night. I think that he finally succeeded though. I see him on TV every so often. I could never have been with him."

"You'll do anything for love?" I asked her.

"Once I met a guy at a club. He was so nice to me and invited me back to his house. When we got there, the guy's girlfriend was in bed. He told me that it would really turn him on if I did it with his girlfriend. I liked the guy, and I had drunk too much, and she was cute. But I only did that once. Now I can't think of anything grosser. But I know it turns guys on when I tell them that story. You'd love to be with two women," she laughed. "But I tell you, it's not going to happen. Not with me anyway. I can't be with two people. I need one person who will love me totally and completely."

One night I sat with Jacqueline and her mother, sharing an Australian botrytis after dinner. Jacqueline excused herself from the table and her mother took advantage of her daughter's absence. "God how I have suffered with that girl. She dropped out of college and spent every night dancing at nightclubs. One night, she met a girl who was gorgeous; she was some kind of model. The girl started coming over to the house, and eventually she started spending the night at our house. She slept in Jacqueline's room and they would lock themselves in there. But the walls aren't that thick. I know what was going on. It went on for over two months. Then the girl would call Jacqueline at two and three in the morning. When I told the girl that she had to stop calling that late, Jacqueline freaked, and broke all my chinaware. God, please don't tell her I told you. She'll go crazy."

"What happened after that?"

"The girl found herself a boyfriend and Jacqueline became very depressed. We were worried and encouraged her to go out more, to start working out. She started to go to a gym and she met another woman who was just as pretty as the first. All her friends are beautiful. I think she does it because her self-esteem is so low. They soon became good friends and they decided to go on a double date. Jacqueline invited a man that she had been keen on. He had said that he would invite a friend, but the friend did not arrive. He spent his whole time talking to the other girl. Jacqueline said that she had to go to the powder room, but instead she came back to the house and got one of my biggest kitchen knives. She went back to the club and slashed the girl's tires. When the girl came out and tried to drive home, she got out of the car to see what the trouble was, but Jacqueline chased her back into the car with the knife. The wheels were destroyed as her friend tried to drive away. Anyway, we paid for the damages, but that poor girl, she must have been terrified by the way Jacqueline had suddenly turned on her. You know, Jacqueline has even threatened me with a knife. With her it's like walking on eggshells. I don't know how you do it." She shuddered as she took a sip of her wine.

Every single one of these stories seemed explainable to me in the context of rejection and disappointment in somebody who loved herself so little and had never been unconditionally assured of love. I would change that. I knew that I loved her and she knew that I loved her.

CHAPTER 9

Suburban Johannesburg
Early November 1984

My mother once told me that the most important lesson she could give me came from the New Testament. "Jesus once told his followers: 'My command is this: Love each other as I have loved you'. His love for us was unconditional, as must ours be for our fellow man," she told me. I was thinking of her words when I drove to Jacqueline's house the day after my final exams.

The sun shone especially brightly that day. I changed into a pair of swimming shorts and headed for the pool. Jacqueline's mother came over, towel in hand, and lay down next to me. "Her father and I have been talking. You really have become part of the family; I mean, you are almost like one of the family. Anyway, we are very worried about Jacqueline. She has become so attached to you. She can't stop talking about you. She cares about you a great deal. You are so good to her and we haven't seen her this happy and relaxed and stable in a long time.'
"And I am happy too."

"Yes, but you are going to be leaving town to do your internship, and you know how she does when she is left alone."

"But she can come and visit me whenever she wants. We talked about that already."

"You know that she can't deal with separation," she continued.

"Yes, but she knows that I love her. Besides, it's a separation only in space, not in heart or mind."

"Anthony, you can't build up her expectations and then take yourself away. That would be cruel, especially now that you know her as well as you do. You've seen her at her worst. Even your professor at the hospital said that she could be in a relationship, but that it would have to be with a saint. You see how happy she is. You are her saint. If you left her, you would be setting us up as well. We would have to pick up the pieces yet again."

"But I am off to do my internship. I can't change that," I protested.

"Just don't leave her, it will destroy her." She left to pour herself a gin and tonic. The day had chilled a little in the afternoon sun.

Something unsettled me about the conversation with Jacqueline's mother. I had no thought of leaving Jacqueline, so what was all this about? I felt that I was being manipulated. Howard had warned me of manipulation by Borderline patients, but he had said nothing about their mothers. It bothered me that she would doubt my intentions. I wondered to myself whether she thought I was using Jacqueline, whether she thought I was just out for a "good time."

When I met Jacqueline, her beauty and her energy had enchanted me, but it was her absolute need to be loved that was most captivating. She was like a flower with some exotic pollen and I was a bee. It was flattering to think that this intriguing woman with such sophisticated tastes and varied life experiences could find me interesting. I could not tell a Monet from a Matisse, a flan from a crème caramel, a Versace from a Gucci. It felt good to be so wanted and needed by her; she had so much to teach me about living. This made it easy to love her and care for her. The matter of the suicide attempt was a remote memory, and one that didn't seem to fit. She made it easy for me to forget just how fragile she was.

CHAPTER 10

University of the Witwatersrand
Johannesburg
Late November 1984

Graduation night was an elegant affair. There was enough pomp to make us believe that we had graduated to godliness. I had invited Jacqueline as my guest, and she sat with my parents, sharing the moment when I could officially add an MD to my name. At the end of the event, my father took me aside with a concerned look on his face. There were so many things in life that he took seriously that his looks of concern held little real significance to me anymore. "Anthony, you have such a whole and exciting life ahead of you. I'm worried that you are getting too involved too quickly, that you will throw away everything that you have worked for before you even have a chance to know all your possibilities and opportunities. I am worried that you are getting so deeply involved with someone you don't even know. I tried to talk to her. She has no goals. She expects you to take care of her. Does she have any idea as to just how busy your year is going to be?" I didn't want to have this discussion with him. I was sure that he would not easily understand how Jacqueline brought me the unpredictability that I wanted in my life.

"Dad, don't worry. I know what I'm doing."

Jacqueline and I drove off to our favorite coffee shop for a long talk over a long coffee. I told her about my dream of becoming a psychiatrist one day. "That's why I went to medical school. I know that the next year is going to be hell with call and everything. I feel so close to you, but this time we have spent together is going to end soon. Your mother is worried that you won't be able to handle me working all that time."

"Thinking of you working so many long hours makes me sad. It makes me so sad that I miss you already and you are still here. I can't take it."

"The first year is the worst, but after that it will become easier, you'll see." She began to cry softly and took my hands.

"How do I know that it will get easier? How do I know that you won't leave me just like everybody else has?

"Look at me. I won't leave you because I love you. I will never leave you, and you have to hold that in your heart." She bowed her head, then softly said, "Men have always told me that they loved me and that they would never leave me, but look at me. I am still alone."

We talked into the night. Eventually the staff asked us to leave. Jacqueline was still not convinced. Her experience had been one of hope followed by rejection at every turn. I wanted to show her that I meant what I was telling her. We headed for the elevator that led to the underground parking. Suddenly it hit me. I knew just what I had to say to prove to her that I loved her: "Jacqueline, will you marry me?" She stopped and looked at me, stunned.

"Do you mean that?"

"Of course I mean it. Once I finish my internship we'll get married. One year, and then we'll do it, what do you say?" The door opened and we entered the elevator. In classical Jacqueline style , she kissed me so passionately and emphatically that her answer was clear.

"Let's make love right here."

"It's a glass elevator," I laughed.

"You really do love me," she said, relieved, and held my arm tight.

When we got back to her parents' house some time after midnight, she could not wait to tell her mother. She ran excitedly down the hall to their room. The talk in the bedroom was animated, and I paced nervously back and forth in the parlor. "He what?" I heard her mother shout out. "Is he drunk?"

"No, mom, we haven't had anything to drink. Really, he asked me."

"Alright dear, we'll talk about it in the morning." Jacqueline returned smiling, and then hugged me. "Thank you for believing in me." I went home with the peace of mind that Jacqueline could finally be certain about my sincerity. Everything would be all right now.

Jacqueline's mother dealt with her incredulity the way that she dealt with most other things in her life. "Let's have a party! Why don't you each invite some friends? Anthony, I'll cook a meal that will move even your dad." Jacqueline's mother ran a cooking school which had been successful for over thirty years. Her daughter's engagement party brought out the height of her culinary skills. Immediately she got to work on the menu. First a salad of cherry tomatoes, fresh basil, chopped fresh parsley and minced garlic on Romaine lettuce dressed with a homemade mayonnaise. Freshly baked baguettes would accompany the entire meal. Following would be a whole lamb on the spit, which would be continuously basted with a marinade of oil, vinegar, mustard, garlic, salt, pepper, ginger, cumin, paprika and rosemary. "The 1979 Arrowood Chardonnay will be in ample supply," her father had insisted.

"So will Perrier," laughed Jacqueline. Dessert would be a Chocolat Poiver accompanied by a Sauterne that her father had picked out.

Amidst the preparations, I had yet to confront the hard part; telling my family, especially my father. I went for long walks and had many imaginary conversations with him. I would think of what he would say and then would argue with him. He would make a point and then I a counterpoint. Even though the conversation was imagined, I could never get him to agree with me. Still, I had to tell him. One day he came back from work in a particularly cheery mood. This would have to be the time. "Dad, I need to talk to you…"

"You what????"

"I know exactly what you think, I have gone over this conversation a thousand times in my head. But it is a matter of judgment, and I know that everything is going to come out alright."

"I have only met her three times. How can you know what I think? I don't even know what I think." He was upset and stood up from his chair. "Can't you see that in this relationship, all that you are ever going to do is give? What will you ever get back? Love is a two-way affair. If all that you wanted was a piece of ass, you could get that anywhere." He was becoming desperate, maybe even angry.

"You don't understand, Dad. She has never been loved, not really loved. She has so much potential as a person, but she has been consumed her entire life by loathing and self-doubt. She never knew the kind of love that you guys gave us."

"So what you want to do is to parent her?"

"Dad, once she realizes what it means to be loved, and once she feels loved, all her insecurities will disappear and she will shine."

"I still don't get it. You are marrying her out of pity? How long will it take until she gets it? What if it takes a lifetime?"

"I know that she loves me. She makes me feel like my love is worth something. The whole thing is very intense."

"You know, you are so much like your mother. You take in the weak of the world and end up getting screwed."

"Really, who is happier? You or mom?"

"We don't even know her parents."

"That is something that I can take care of," I said, grateful to end the discussion. I called Jacqueline and told her that we had to set up a meeting between our parents. They were so different. The religion of fish on Fridays was about to meet the religion of haute cuisine and vintage wine.

I had set the meeting up for a Saturday afternoon, when Jacqueline's mother was not teaching class and my father would have wound down from the week's work. Her father uncharacteristically wore a tie and my father characteristically did as well. Their greetings were respectful but awkward. We left the house and went back to hers. When we got to the house we wondered what they were saying. We role-played each other's parents, accentuating their idiosyncrasies, laughing nervously all the while. Her parents were there for hours but eventually they returned. "We were honest and they were cordial. You have nice parents." I was relieved, but they wouldn't say more. I didn't believe that my father had not put up a fight.

When I got home my father was sitting in his armchair. He was tugging at his chin, staring into space the way he does when he has something deep to think about. I knew that he had been waiting for me. He held his hands together as if in prayer. "Anthony, I know that your mind is made up. I want you just to spend some time thinking about how mentally ill she is. She tried to commit suicide. She is impulsive and unpredictable. And more than that, they are a family without God. She is going to need a lifetime of treatment. You are not going to marry a life partner, but somebody who is going to need your care for the rest of her life. If you still decide that you are going to marry her I will not stand in your way. I strongly disapprove. Please think about it. Your mother and I truly love you." I kissed him and hugged him.

"Thanks, dad."

"OK," he said resignedly. "We'll get through it somehow."

I felt relieved, intensely relieved. I wanted to put his feelings out of my mind. I phoned Jacqueline, "Hey, squirrel, let's celebrate." I had started calling her squirrel for the way that she tucked herself into bed at night. She took the duvet and wrapped it around her body, then covered her head so that only her face and hands, holding the duvet, were visible, like a squirrel peering out of a hole in a tree. "Squirrels need a lot of love and a lot of warmth," she had instructed me. "I am going to be your squirrel." We decided to make an unofficial and surprise announcement of our engagement to our close friends at a favorite restaurant. After the first round of drinks were served, I stood up and said, "Jacqueline and I have decided to get married. If you will raise your glass to Jacqueline." All of her friends erupted into laughter and joy, congratulating her heartily. My friends congratulated me as well, but not with the usual happiness associated with such an occasion. After a few drinks, my friends warmed up to the idea more, but the drink also loosened their inhibitions. Gary was the most critical.

I had known Gary since the day we had met at registration on the first day of medical school. Now, after graduation, we were able to reflect on the entire course of our journey from pre-meds to qualified doctors. We had done so much together between studying, partying, playing bridge, traveling and dreaming. One time we decided to run a marathon together. Anybody who ran it in under four-and-a-half hours would get a medal, but even more importantly, would qualify for the infamous 58-mile Comrades Marathon. After I had finished, I went back to look for Gary who was still on the course. I looked at the race clock and it showed four hours and nineteen minutes. I ran out of the stadium and found him a mile from the finish line, not wanting to go on. "Come on, Gary. Eleven minutes. You can do it!"
"I'm stuffed. My legs are cramping, I'm hungry, and I had to stop to take a dump a mile back. There is no way. Now I just want to finish." I knew

that this was not true. He had been so set on finishing in under the required time that he had taken bets at school.

"Gary, you are going to run if I have to boot you across the finish line." He laughed and started to trot. "Come on. A little faster, you're nearly there." We were nearing the stadium. "Gary, you have wanted this so badly, you will be so upset with yourself if you don't do it. You have been suffering for nearly four-and-a-half hours. Five minutes more won't kill you now." We entered the stadium. "A quarter mile, Gary. You have two and a half minutes." The race marshal told me to get off the course as I had already finished. Gary was on his own. He collapsed across the finish line. His time was four hours, twenty-nine minutes and fifty-six seconds. He had made it; the officials gave him his medal as the medics helped him to the recovery tent.

Gary and I had been there for each other during our entire medical training. We understood the things that mattered to each other. At the restaurant, that evening, he pulled me aside. "We are happy for you, if you are, but I know you. You never wanted this. Your dream will end. Remember that book you gave me? *Illusions*, by Richard Bach? She isn't your soul mate. Yes, she is gorgeous, but her head is screwed up."

"Gary, I invited you here not to fight. I want you to be happy for me and for us. Her head is something that I understand. She is more alive than anyone that I have ever known."

"Just how alive is she? She nearly killed herself."

"Gary, get serious."

"I am serious, my friend, but this is something that I see you are going to have to work out on your own." He started to drink. Eventually somebody drove him home. The dissent had ended.

The next morning she woke up earlier than usual. "There is just one last thing left to do before our formal party. I want a ring," said Jacqueline. "A ring will make it official. I want to show it off."

"And you will have one. Let's go look today." We cruised the jewelers at a high-end shopping center, looking at the diamonds in their display cabinets. "God, can you ever imagine wearing one of those tiny pieces of shit," she said derisively of a smaller stone. It bothered me that the size of the diamond meant so much to her. She knew that my father disapproved of the wedding and that he would not help me in this endeavor. I would pay for the ring myself. In my pre-internship year, I had been paid a "travel-stipend" of a hundred dollars a month, hardly enough to cover the cost of a large diamond. As if she had read my mind, she said, "Baby, I know what you are giving up to do this for me, but I want you to know that I will always be able to look at it when you are not with me, and know just how much you care, just how much you sacrificed." Later that day her mother told me that they had a relative in the jewelry business, and that he would get me something at cost. Jacqueline got her ring.

CHAPTER 11

I enjoy being in situations that make me laugh so hard and long that my stomach hurts and my eyes water. I have always found humor to be a great reliever of stress, and other than studying, the two things that got me through the six years of medical school were friendships and humor.

We had a very serious colleague in our second-year class. She had recently moved to South Africa from France. She told us that she was serious only because she had to concentrate on the lectures as she had a difficult time understanding English. During human dissection, a course that lasted a year and involved four medical students dissecting in its entirety a donated human cadaver, she would complain bitterly when the body she was examining varied in the slightest from the pictures in the anatomy book we were using. One evening, on the day before we were to begin the examination of the intestines, we snuck into the dissection hall and removed a small section of bowel from our cadaver, and stitched it on to the bowel of her cadaver. The next day all hell erupted from the neighboring table as she ran around shouting that her book had nothing about extra bits of bowel attached to the gut. The senior anatomist teaching the course quickly discovered the prank and gave a stern lecture on the need to respect these human remains. Later

our French colleague was able to laugh at the incident, and she stopped
taking herself so seriously.

The third year was the last purely academic year. At the end of the year
we learned the elements of stitching up a wound. To this end we prac-
ticed on an orange, which we were told had a similar 'give' to human
skin. Later, after we were done with the third year exams, Gary took me
to Durban in order to teach me surfing. "This beach will be good,
because the waves are not so big. A lot of beginners start here," he
assured me. While he was showing me the technique of ducking under a
breaking wave, one of the beginners accidentally rammed the point of
his surfboard into Gary's protruding rear-end. He screamed in pain and
turned white. The surfer and I held on to Gary's board and paddled him
to shore. Fortunately, we were able to get him seen at a beachfront clinic.
"So you guys are med students?" asked the attending doctor. We con-
firmed that we had just finished third year, so he offered me the needle
and thread. "Why don't you stitch up your friend?"
"What do you think, Gary?" I asked him.
"C'est la vie," he replied in his usual relaxed way. Gary lay on his stomach as I cleaned the wound and prepared the needle.
"OK, here goes," I warned him, inexpertly inserting the needle into the
edge of the cut.
"Yooooooouch," he shouted nearly jumping off the table, "what the hell
was that?" The doctor came in.
"What happened?" Then he noticed the unopened vial of anesthetic
lying in the suture tray. "Don't you think that he'll need some of this?"
he laughed. This being my first experience on a living human subject, I
hadn't thought of it. The orange and the cadaver had never complained.
After that incident my friendship with Gary was sealed, and we would
spend many post-study hours playing bridge and drinking our favorite
Nederburg Cabernet Sauvignon.

Aside from Gary and my bridge-playing, wine-drinking friends, Aaron was my closest confidante. I trusted him, literally, with my life. Together we had signed up for, and completed, a parachute jump. He was a restless adventurer, seldom content with routine. We had gone to medical school together, but halfway through he quit to go and hike in Nepal. For him it was always about the experience. He was an excellent athlete and we spent many an hour running through the streets of Johannesburg chatting about girlfriends, rugby, movies, black holes and the solutions to life's problems. After months of training with him, and having earlier qualified for it, he proposed running the Comrades Marathon. In May of my fourth year, we ran the race together. I finished the monster course, which wound uphill climbing over nineteen hundred feet from Durban to Pietermaritzburg, in just over ten hours, and lived to tell the tale. Although Aaron had an opinion on many things, he was always non-judgmental about my personal choices, unlike Gary who told me exactly what he thought of everything I did. Perhaps I should have asked Aaron early on what he thought about my relationship with Jacqueline, but because I didn't expect an opinion, I didn't ask him. I had left one of my closest confidantes without a voice.

Dating was a frivolous affair for many of us during medical school. There did not seem to be enough time or energy to commit to serious relationships. The nursing students and the medical students played the same game with each other, and usually after a few movies and a brief romance each moved on. It was more difficult to date during the surgery rotations, because of the long hours in the operating room, and the frequency of the call, so we all looked forward to the easier rotations like dermatology and ophthalmology.

It was the mix of study, friendship and laughter that made it possible to get sanely through medical school, and even though I knew that the crazy and long hours would come to an end, I still looked forward to maintaining this balance, long after school had ended.

CHAPTER 12

Suburban Johannesburg
Early December 1984

After I had completed the final examinations at medical school, Jacqueline and I spent nearly all our time together. There were two nights when she told me that she couldn't make it to one of the many graduation parties, so I met up with friends instead. On both of those occasions she showed up at the party some time later, and to my great delight. "How did you know where we were?" I asked her.

"You weren't thinking that you could get away from me that easily, were you?" she laughed.

"As if I'd ever want to," I laughed with her. "Besides, I'm glad you came. I want everyone to know why I am so happy."

As graduation was over, we turned our attention to the engagement party. Jacqueline's mother had set the menu, so we were instructed to order the chairs, tables, stemware and flatware. The running around and preparing for the party felt in some ways like running away for me. I was distracted from thinking about what I was doing, and from my father's antipathy. I knew that he felt that I hadn't given his earlier warning, much thought. In the mornings, I stayed in bed until after he had left for work so that I wouldn't have to face him over the breakfast table and deal with his objections. In the evenings I left before he returned home, and I left my bedroom window open so that I could get in at night. I knew how much he was opposed to what I was about to do. But I also knew that there was no convincing him of the fact that I had made a decision that I was prepared to live by. He was the immovable object and Jacqueline the irresistible force. I could not tolerate the tension between, on the one hand, his total rejection of her and what he felt she represented, and on the other, her need to not have me fail and abandon her. I had made my choice, and she was my future. I felt that in time he would understand.

During the day, I would be with Jacqueline at her house. We helped her mother with the garden, with polishing the silver, and with ensuring that the crystal wine glasses were free of blemish. There was not a spot in the house that did not receive attention. "Great food demands a great presentation," her mother insisted. Soon, the day was upon us.

The party began in the late afternoon of a warm summer's day. The sky was an immaculate blue—even that detail seemed to have been taken care of. The lawn was manicured, without so much as a single dandelion to spoil it. The garden bloomed with white dendrobiums, deep pink peonies, and petunias. The pool obediently mirrored the blue of the sky. At the door the guests were greeted with Veuve-Clicquot in Baccarat flutes. Pockets of people began to form and dissolve as we moved from one "congratulations" to the next. My parents had not yet arrived, so I numbed my anxiety with Chardonnay. When this did not help, I took an offered cigarette with no remorse. When still they had not arrived, anxiety became anger at their rudeness, but even that passed, and by the time they showed up the party had swung into full disinhibition. The last rays of the late-afternoon sun invited all to a last look at the garden.

My father wore a solemn suit to this solemn occasion. He sought out a glass of wine to numb his pain and then sought out Gary to commiserate with, but other than this pessimistic couple all the other guests seemed to be enjoying themselves. Jacqueline's therapist had been invited, and upon arrival the therapist cornered me and commended me on how well Jacqueline was doing. "You're all she talks about in therapy. You have surprised all of us with your tenacity. You'll need it. Jacqui is one tough girl." I wondered if she was warning me, but could see no hint of this in her face. A loud drone of relaxed chatter filled the evening. Laughter and merriment drowned out any lingering feelings of doubt. An occasional knife clinked on the side of an empty wineglass to propose a toast, and we cheered and laughed. Her father spoke of how much they had come to love me and how happy Jacqueline seemed to be. "I don't recall her ever having been so content with life and with herself." My father uncharacteristically, but not unexpectedly, made no speech. I filled the silence. "When two people meet, and have feelings for each other, it is usual that each shows the other all the niceness about themselves. Seldom do we bare our weaknesses in the initial encounters for fear of driving the other away. It is later that these flaws are revealed and the core of the relationship is truly tested. When I met Jacqueline, as all of you know, she was in the hospital, hopeless and in pain. It is easy to love someone who is perfect, but Jacqueline allowed me to share in her weakest moment, and Squirrel, I love you for that, and nothing will ever break that love apart." Hooting and whistling accompanied Jacqueline's passionate kiss.

"Everything is going to be just perfect. I promise you," she whispered.

CHAPTER 13

My internship would begin in a month. I had matched my first choice, Katatura Hospital in Windhoek. Windhoek is a desert town, a thousand miles away from Johannesburg, on the barren Atlantic coast of Africa in the country of Namibia. It was a thousand miles away from my parents and hers, a thousand miles away from managed care and crowded emergency rooms, a thousand miles away from big-city violence and full parking lots.

My car was an old red Ford Mustang. The muffler didn't quite muffle, but it was impossible to find the right part. The dogs could hear it coming a mile from the house. Getting the car ready for the trip was as much an act of mercy as it was of necessity. Two weeks before we were to leave, I received a call from the director of housing at Katatura, informing me that she had arranged a studio apartment for me in their doctors' apartment block, and that the caretaker would have a key. I told her that I would need a larger apartment as I was just engaged and that my fiancée would be staying with me. "But you did not indicate that on your application form," she said.

"Well, it was all rather sudden," I explained.

"We reserve all the bigger apartments for the married couples and those with kids. I am sorry, but housing is tight for the doctors. If you would like we could look for something in town. We can't guarantee anything, though." The original housing offer had sounded ideal as it offered all the amenities that a sleep, exercise, and food-deprived intern could ask for. Moreover, it was on the hospital grounds, and would be far less expensive than a private rent, so a move into town was not appealing.

"What assholes," said Jacqueline. Her mind worked quickly. We had previously agreed to have a traditional wedding after my internship was over. "Let's just tell them that we are married."
"I told her that we are engaged, and that we were getting married next year. She said that there was no way that they could provide a bigger apartment, unless we are married or have kids."
"They want us to be married? Let's just go down to the courthouse and get married. We won't tell anybody, so next year we'll still get our wedding and for now we will have a bigger apartment."

Our relationship had reached a sudden and critical juncture. I had felt that the decision to wait a year before we got married made sense so that we could see what living together would bring, especially during a year of internship with multiple demands on my time. Also I wanted to show my father that I had spent time thinking about what I was doing, to show him that Jacqueline and I could be a couple, and ultimately get his blessing. But if we did not go through with Jacqueline's plan, she would not be able to live with me in Windhoek, and there was no way our relationship would last. "I need to be with you. I can't stay here in Johannesburg and you there. If you abandon me, I'll have to look for somebody else. I can't be alone. You know that." I had made a commitment to her. I felt that I had no choice. I would not abandon her. I telephoned the local justices-of-the-peace, but due to the short notice, nobody in our town could marry us. Jacqueline then called, and found a minister in the next town who told us that their civil court performed weddings on Wednesdays and that he had just had a cancellation. He would be glad to submit our names instead. We immediately took the offer. All we needed was two witnesses and twenty-five dollars. I imagined what my father would say. "A marriage without God is not a marriage."

Because Aaron knew me as well as he did, I finally wondered aloud what he thought of my relationship with Jacqueline. He told me that he felt that my romance was just another adventure. "Just like jumping out of an airplane or running the Comrades marathon, the experience will change your life no matter what the outcome," he assured me.

"OK, my friend, I want you to be part of this experience, just like all the others we have shared. Jacqueline and I were going to wait a year to get married, but we have to do it immediately in order to get housing in Windhoek," I told him. "I want you to be my witness and best man. Be there by eleven on the Wednesday, and please Aaron, don't tell anybody. If my father ever finds out, it will kill him."

"I have a meeting which ends at ten thirty. I'll be there on time, and don't worry, no one will know, at least not from me."

I cannot say that I did not have lingering doubts over the next few days. The reality of what I was about to do made me think and reflect on the events of the past few months. Jacqueline and I had known each other for two and a half months. We had been engaged for two weeks and were to be married in a few days. I didn't believe I could put the wedding on hold. It would have shattered Jacqueline's fragile but growing sense of trust and hope. But I dreaded going through with it a year before I had intended, and just for the sake of the apartment. Our relationship had yet to be put to any significant test. Finally I decided that there was no choice for me but to stand by a conviction.

Wednesday morning arrived, and we got to court shortly before the eleventh hour. A receptionist showed us to a small, sparsely decorated, windowless room, which had a large, formal-looking chair and solid wood table at one end, and four folding-chairs leaning against the wall at the other. The South African national flag hung behind the table, and was the only symbol of officialdom. "Just take the two middle chairs, and when your witnesses arrive, tell them to take the other two chairs," said the receptionist. Jacqueline's friend Kathy arrived, but shortly after eleven there was still no sign of Aaron. An elderly woman peered around the door. "Sorry dears, we are going to have to start. The next couple is waiting." I asked her to wait for another minute but Aaron did not show. Instead the judge walked in with jeans showing under an ill-fitting gown, carrying a large, red leather-bound book. "We are going to have to start. Is your witness here?" Aaron had still not arrived. "You will need a witness. There is a secretary pool down the hall. Ask one of them to stand in for your friend." A kind but bored woman in her mid-thirties offered to be witness. "It's the first time that I have ever been a best man," she laughed, and then the ceremony was conducted. By the power invested in the judge, we were pronounced husband and wife. "Please sign here," he said, opening up the red book, "and pay the cashier on the way out." And then he was gone. In the waiting room a young couple sat, hands and eyes interlocked, waiting for their ten minutes in court. We paid the cashier and I looked at my watch. 11:08. There was still no sign of Aaron, so after a few more minutes we left. Kathy had a cold bottle of Moet waiting for us her the car, a Volkswagen Golf, and she had offered to be our chauffer for the day. She drove us to a trendy French restaurant while we polished off the champagne in the back the car. At lunch, we sat in a secluded booth and ordered Chardonnay by the bottle, which we accompanied with oysters by the plateful. Then, hardly needing a main course, we ordered that too. Jacqueline placed an oyster in her mouth, and then took my hand, sucking on my fingers with the oyster, still smooth, in her mouth. She then took my hand and placed it gently between her thighs and slowly rubbed herself on it. She reached orgasm just as the waiter brought our dessert, a slice of Black Forest cake. "Another plate of oysters," said Jacqueline.

"After the chocolate, madam?" queried the waiter.

"Yes," Jacqueline laughed. "But then wait twenty minutes before bringing the coffee."

CHAPTER 14

The next morning, I awoke hung over. "I'm married," I said to myself, as if this were a sudden revelation. I decided to go for a jog. Jogging had been my mainstay exercise for over three years, and I had managed to maintain my weight at around a hundred and seventy pounds for the past few years. But with the excitement of a new romance, the restaurants, the year-end parties and Jacqueline's mother's cooking, jogging had slipped down on my priority list. That morning I stood on the scale, and one hundred and eighty pounds stared me straight in the gut. I moved the scale around to make sure that the error was not a placement error but the weight did not change. My new, food-rich lifestyle had taken its toll. I had to put a quick stop to the weight gain. "I am off, darling," I told Jacqueline, who lay burrowed in her duvet.

"Where to?" she asked.

"For a run. Look at this, I am getting fat." I wobbled my gut in front of her, laughing.

'So what?"

"What do you mean?"

"So what if you're getting fat?"

"I need to lose some weight."

"Who are you trying to impress?"

"Nobody, it's just a healthy thing to do. Anyway, my pants are getting tight."

"What's wrong with all you men? You think that you have to have rock hard bodies to get the chicks. That's not what women want. That's not what I want. I want you to take care of me. I want you to make so much money that I never have to work, and that we can go to restaurants whenever we want. I don't want some pansy prancing around in his tights."

"What's gotten into you? This isn't some vanity trip. I'm just going for a run."

"So it is more important to you to go for a run than to be with me?"

"What are you talking about? I am with you. I'll be back in half an hour." Jacqueline took a half-empty wineglass from the nightstand and smashed it to the ground. "What the hell are you doing to me? You promised me that you would never leave." I shuddered and stepped back from her. She started to cry. "You are doing that now. You promised that you would never leave me." I went to hold her.

"I promise you baby that I will never leave you. If it means so much to you, I won't go for the run today. It's no big deal."

"Just promise me that you will never leave me."

"I promise," I said sincerely.

"Let's go lie by the pool. I want to bring you something." She disappeared, and then returned sometime later carrying two large bowls of ice cream that she had decorated with cherries and a banana to make a smiling face. "I love you."

"I love you too."

CHAPTER 15

"I have something for you," Jacqueline proclaimed triumphantly one morning.

"What is it?" I wondered.

"Close your eyes," she said playfully, then covered my eyes with her hand to be sure that I didn't peek. She led me into the hallway and faced me toward the far end of the hall. "Keep them closed," she ordered, and then removed her hand from my face. I heard her walk away. "OK, now open them." On the far wall a sheet covered the clear outline of a large frame. She pulled the sheet off the painting.

From behind the sheet appeared an oil, painted on canvas. She had had it framed in an intricate solid wood frame. I stared at the painting for a long time, to take it all in. Jacqueline had created a Chagall-like flower arrangement which overflowed with yellow lilies, white chrysanthemums, blue irises, yellow and white alstroemeria, and with baby's breath flowing from a rustic clay pot. The background was a fiery sunset red that made the piece look larger than it was.

"That could hang in any gallery anywhere in the world. It is magnificent," I said finally. "When did you have time to do it?"

"I started on it soon after we met. I had a lot of time to work on it during your exams. I wanted to show you that I had been thinking of you all this time. Also, I'm sorry about the other day."

I was sure that the mind that had created such art was close to genius. Van Gogh and Michelangelo had all been excused for their madness. I was not in their presence, but Jacqueline was as close as I would get to artistic greatness. Perhaps she needed her rage to create. It was a small price to pay for such beauty.

CHAPTER 16

The next few days were spent preparing the last details of the trip. The tension at my parents' home was intolerable. My father hoped that I would change my mind. He asked my friends to speak to me, but my mind was made up. Even more significantly, although he did not know it, Jacqueline and I were legally married. I could not wait to leave.

Soon the day arrived, and with the car packed we said our good-byes to her parents and drove to my parents' home. After she had wished Jacqueline luck, my mother hugged her and cried. My father hugged me and said softly, "Just remember that no matter what happens, we will always be there for you." We got in the car and Jacqueline turned on the radio. Meatloaf was singing '*Bat out of Hell.*'

We left the city and drove through the suburbs and then on to the stretches of open road between the towns and then into the desert. Greens faded into dry summer browns as we entered the semi-arid Karoo region of the western Transvaal-province. We passed through the border-post into Namibia. The alien rock-formations of the Namib Desert broke the monotony of the straight shimmering blacktop. The car had no air-conditioning and the fan blew hot engine-air back into the car. After we had reached no particular place, we stopped, stripped down to our shorts and walked out onto the desert sands. Our bodies glistened with the moisture of sweat. We danced deliriously in the sun to the sound of the distant car radio. A lizard appeared, then quickly darted back into the shade of a small rock. We headed back to the car. The ice that had kept the Coke cold was now tepid water at the bottom of the ice chest, but even that brought some relief as we poured the water over ourselves. We continued the drive through the late afternoon and watched as the sun finally set behind a large mesa. Mercifully the night came quickly and took the heat away, even bringing with it an occasional breeze. Suddenly over a rise, the lights of a town appeared. The familiar sign of a Holiday Inn promised air-conditioned rooms and ice-cold beer. We settled for both.

The next morning we continued west and reached a gravel road with a sign that promised to take a hundred miles off the trip. The surface looked to be in good condition, so we left the paved national-road and headed into the brush. Twenty miles into the desert we realized how absolutely alone we were. The only sign of civilization was the ever-deteriorating road we were driving on. After a long silence, Jacqueline said suddenly, "This is what it is like sometimes. I am alone in an empty world that I can't even recognize. It's better to be dead." The times that she was able to reflect on her life were rare. Usually, after she had had an outburst, she would yell and shout about how miserable her life was, and how she would rather be dead. This moment was different. Unprovoked and reflective, she told it the way that it was for her. I put my hand on her bare knee and gave her a reassuring squeeze.

After a while the road rejoined the interstate. The gravel road had been in such poor condition that we had added another two hours to the trip, but eventually, after another hundred miles, we reached the outer limits of Windhoek. A gas station attendant directed us to the other end of the town where the hospital was. "Fifty thousand people live in the area," he said, almost proudly. We continued on to the hospital and found the doctors' living quarters well sign-posted. An older, heavyset woman answered my knock on the caretaker's door. "Apartment 2B," she pointed us to some stairs. "You go up that way, and I'll take the elevator." She met us at the top of the stairs and led us to our new home. The apartment had two bedrooms, a living room, kitchen and a bathroom. The place was empty except for two single beds separated by a small bookstand, and a refrigerator in the kitchen.

"Where's the air conditioner? Where's the double bed?" asked Jacqueline.

"None of the apartments are air-conditioned," said the caretaker.

"How do people take the heat?" I persisted, perspiring.

"This is the desert. We have always lived with the heat. If you want an air conditioner, you can go into town and buy one. And you can get a double bed there too, if you want one."

We moved the bookstand and pushed the beds together, then left for town to buy bedding for two singles, food to stock the refrigerator, and to look for an air conditioner. The first two tasks were a success. The last proved impossible, as the summer's early heat had ensured a complete depletion of any stocks. An order would take a couple of weeks. Instead we bought a large water-cooled fan. That first night I dreamt that I had built a sauna in the middle of the desert and had sat in it fully clothed, unable to get out.

The next day was the last free day before my internship began. We woke early. Jacqueline filled the ice-trays with water and placed them in the freezer. "I'll show you why later," she said suggestively. We then drove into town to get our bearings. We stopped at the bank to open an account and get a loan in order to buy furniture for the apartment. Jacqueline found a classic dining-room table with four chairs in unfinished oak, so we put our loan to immediate use. Happy with our purchase we next found the only European style restaurant in town. It offered fresh oysters and we sat down to a plateful, accompanied by a chilled Zinfandel. Both had their desired effect and we rushed back in the midday heat to an ice-cold bath, using the ice from the freezer. Jacqueline turned on the radio. Sinatra was singing '*For once in my life.*' She sang along:

> ...*I've got someone who needs me*
> *Someone I've needed so long*
> *For once unafraid I can go where life leads me*
> *And somehow I know I'll be strong*

Finally, frozen and lightheaded, we warmed our bodies in love and whispered to each other that we would overcome any obstacle and be together forever.

CHAPTER 17

Windhoek, Namibia
January 1985

The next day I arrived early at the hospital and met my colleagues. All but one of the new interns had graduated from South African medical schools. One woman had studied in Russia and barely spoke English, but she appeared just as excited and nervous as the rest of us. The attending staff divided us into groups of two and handed us a schedule for the rest of the year. I also received a pager and, oddly, it was only after attaching it to my belt that I felt fully confident that I was an official doctor.

The paging system that the hospital used was a voice activated system and had a 10-mile radius. It immediately announced the caller's message. The hospital operator would preface the message with "Doctor" and all nearby could hear. "Doctor, you are needed in Ward Three-B to replace a leaking catheter." The first few times I looked around to see whether people had noticed, but after a few days the pager became more of a nuisance than a status symbol. In truth, though, I was terrified of the new responsibility, unsure of whether anything that I had learned in medical school would be of practical use.

My first assignment was a two-month stint in a surgery rotation. This required my being at the hospital by six in the morning and getting home by six at night. I spent the day in the operating room. Every third night I was on-call for the surgery service, and I slept, though barely so, in the doctor's quarters at the hospital.

Jacqueline soon began to hate life in Windhoek. She was unable to escape from her own insecurities through the activity that had filled her life in Johannesburg. She could no longer spend time cruising the malls, having coffees in quaint coffee shops, and talking to friends over lunch, for there were no malls or coffee shops or friends. With these gone, she had little to do but think about her life. The solitude forced her to face the fears that haunted her most; her fear of abandonment and her fear of being alone. The loneliness magnified her feeling of emptiness. She knew that this life style would eventually make her snap. She would lose control and lash out, then feel embarrassed for having done so. She always hated herself after losing control. She so hated that part of her psyche that could not control the anger that the thought of dying during those moments was, for her, relieving. "If I killed myself I wouldn't have to live with myself, and I wouldn't end up hurting so many people."

"I know that you hate being here, but you have no threats here," I reassured her. "I have no family and friends to take me away from you." She had me all to herself.

"Yes, but your job takes you away from me for 12 hours a day, sometimes more. And you aren't the only one without friends. Imagine what it is like for me just having to sit here and wait." She had lost her motivation to paint, but one Saturday afternoon we found a private pottery class. She dropped out after one lesson. "You just want me to do pottery lessons so that you can spend some time away from me. It's your way of driving me away," she told me one day. "In any case, I really hate it here. There is nothing to do. I can't even get a job." She was right about the job because a proficiency in Afrikaans or German was necessary for employment in this once German colony. She spoke neither.

"You knew that when we moved here, you decided to make the move in any case, to be here with me," I chided her. The reality of the dreary day-to-day life in the desert had killed the motivation that she had shown before the trip. She spent her time in the apartment reading and waiting for me to come home. In the evenings we ate out, although there wasn't much variety. One night we found an eccentric restaurant run by a large German man and his tiny wife. Both shared a booming laugh and readily accepted an invitation to share a beer, but the novelty of eating there soon wore off. The only cinema in town changed their feature every three weeks, but fortunately there was a good video-rental store a few blocks from the apartment.

On the weekends that I was not on call, we would go exploring the Namib. These trips cheered her up a lot. She prepared a picnic basket full of cheese, cold cuts, bread, and wine and we would set off to discover a new aspect of the desert. One afternoon we unexpectedly found a small lake, a feature that did not appear on our map. It was more of a pond, but a sign identified it as the "largest body of water in the Windhoek area." A large rock at its edge made it an ideal place to hide from the heat and enjoy a picnic. It was under that rock that we got down to the work of really knowing each other. We would talk and fight for hours about our dreams and ourselves. This was the process that I had expected to complete during our year of living together, before our sudden marriage.

There were two fundamental areas where we disagreed. The first was that I wanted children and she did not. "I am sick. I can't even take care of myself. How do you expect me to take care of a child? I want to be your baby. I want you to take care of me like I was your child. Unconditional love is what I need. I love you so much that I just can't stand the idea of sharing your love with anybody else. I want it all to myself. I would go crazy. Maybe I'd even hurt the baby. I know how I get. Why should a baby suffer because of how I am?" she argued.

"When you finally begin to truly believe just how much I love you then maybe we can think about it again. It doesn't have to be now."

"I don't know why people want children. There are already so many in the world and all they do is cry and wet and you can't enjoy yourself. We haven't even started to enjoy our life together and already you are talking about having children and throwing it all away. I want my life to be mine for a while. I have never had that except for now and I want that feeling for a long time."

The second thing that we disagreed on was the importance of family, at least my family. For Jacqueline, it was intolerable that I could love anybody but her. She saw them as a threat to my feelings for her. I could love her and only her. The more I loved my family, the more she hated them. "It is a different kind of love, built over years of being a family. I love you as my wife and my companion and nothing will break that."

"Your family is your past. I am your present and your future. I don't want to hear about your past and your family," she screamed one morning under the rock by the lake.

I could understand why she did not want to have children, but her hatred of my family was intolerable. She attacked them because she knew that she could get me to respond when no other of her provocations would. They were my vulnerability. It became a cycle, her venom towards them and my defending them, which in turn enraged her all the more. She could not tolerate the possibility that I could have any happiness outside of being with her. In her eyes everything in my past was no longer part of me. "I don't want to hear about your life before you met me. It doesn't exist. It is not a part of us. If you were so happy with your family," she would add in a sarcastic, goading tone, "then why are you with me?"

"I was happy then and I am happy now. This is a different stage in my life." The more we didn't see my family, the more fearsome and loathsome they became in her mind. The thought of them was like a cancer that grew unabated. Without being with them she could not see them as good in any way. She saw them as trying to destroy us and destroy her, at every turn. But then, when my mother would call, speaking to her would ground Jacqueline. Jacqueline could feel my mother's compassion. "Maybe your mother is not so bad, but it's your father. What has he ever done for us?"

It was a double-edged sword. On the one hand, she didn't want me to talk about my family and my past. She wanted me to have no identity outside of her. She feared that it would destroy us. "If you love them a little, you can't love me totally and completely, because some of your love is for them." On the other hand she could not tolerate the idea of me keeping any secrets from her. "How do you expect me never to talk to you about my family and my past, but at the same time never to keep anything from you? How is that possible? I am who I am because of my past, my life experiences, everything. I didn't grow up in a vacuum." I protested.

"That's your problem."

Once I received a letter from my brother, and I slipped it into the pages of a book I was reading. Jacqueline found it and tore the letter and the book to shreds. "So how long have you been keeping this behind my back? I can't take your little secrets and your lies."

"You don't want to hear me tell you about them, and then when I don't you go crazy. What do you want me to do?" I always had a terrible feeling at times like these. It was as if she had caught me with my hand in the cookie jar, after handing me the cookie jar. Her extreme insecurity and self-doubt were a malignancy that ate away at her sense of reason. She hated herself for her paranoia, yet she needed it. She believed that people eventually would always leave her. This fear tormented her constantly. She spent her days looking for hints to confirm this belief. Even the smallest disagreement turned into what she saw as the end of love. "Everybody always leaves me in the end, don't you know that? I tell you all the time. You will too. How can anybody love me when I can't even love myself? I take the people that I love the most and I hurt them the most. I am so scared you will leave that I want to give you reason to leave me. It is impossible to love me enough."

Chapter 18

Jacqueline's parents had been kind in giving us some money to make the transition to Namibia easier. They called often to see how we were doing. Her mother always wanted to speak to me to see how Jacqueline was doing, and then she wanted to know if I was all right. It dawned on me that they sent money not just to make things easier for us, but easier for them. "Sure," her mother admitted. "It's a break for us too, not having her around. We can live a normal life, but she is still our daughter."

My parents, on the other hand, were not supportive. They still did not know that we were married. Jacqueline relished the idea that one day she would tell my father that his son had not only been deceitful, but that he had not been married in a church. My father did, however, make periodic phone calls and did so one morning about five weeks into the internship. Jacqueline answered the phone. I was in the bathroom shaving when I heard her say, "he doesn't want to talk to you." I suspected that it was my father and went in to the bedroom to take the call. "I don't give a shit what he is to you," Jacqueline continued. "He is my husband, you fucking asshole!"
"Dad?" I had grabbed the phone from her, but the line was dead. I tried his home and work number but he wasn't at either place.

"He deserved it. He never liked me. What has he ever done for me to show me that he cares? What has he ever done for us? You are with me now. You have to give up your daddy. Don't fight it. He is a grown man. He can take it and so can you." I felt the pain of his having found out that we were married. I was overwhelmed with sadness on my way to work and I cried, not with anger or frustration, but with pity for myself and for being so stupid. I was certain that my father thought that he had lost me for good. I wanted to reach out and tell him that I would be OK, and that I wouldn't allow this relationship to destroy me, or my love for him. I didn't know how to reach out.

When I returned home that evening Jacqueline had prepared a pasta primavera with asparagus. The day had been particularly long in the operating room, as we had nearly lost a patient who had ruptured his spleen in a car accident. I was in no mood to fight with Jacqueline, but she was conciliatory. She hugged me tightly. "I am sorry baby. You know that I love you. I am sorry for the way that I am."

A week went by without anger. In order to make the apartment more attractive, we had decided to sponge paint the walls. This gave Jacqueline a creative task to do for us. She worked hard at it and the tension that had grown between us eased. Fights were inevitably followed by love-making. The passions were extreme. Anger turned to love so fully that it was difficult to imagine that there had ever been anger. For Jacqueline it was the only way to be sure that I really loved her. "I know that you love me because you still make love to me even after we have had a fight." She was right. Her sorrow and embarrassment at her outbursts were real, and her attempts to control her anger so earnest, that I knew she was trying for me, for herself, and for us. I had to remind myself that I had known that she was mentally unstable and that her struggle was my struggle. We would share anger, but we would also share love.

One morning after a particularly hot night the sticky air made us both irritable. Jacqueline was not happy, but I had to leave for work and had little time to sympathize.

"OK, I am off to rounds," I said, indifferently.

"I just can't stand it here," she said.

'Look, this place is the way it is. It's not going to change." I headed for the door, picking up my lab-coat on the way.

"What are you doing to me? Why are you leaving? I'm not doing well. Just stay a little while," she cried.

"We'll talk about it when I get back. I'm late."

"I swear, if you leave now I will kill myself." She sounded desperate.

"I am just going to do rounds. I'll be back in a couple of hours." I picked up my pager and left. As soon as I got into the car, my pager went off.

"Please come back." Her voice was altered electronically by the paging system and she sounded robot-like. I ignored her page, and headed off to the hospital. "Please don't leave," she pleaded over the pager. She paged me three more times on my way in. Each time she was begging, imploring, beseeching that I come back. I started rounds and my pager went off again. "Please call me." Her voice sounded thin yet chilling. She sounded desperate. I excused myself from rounds, and called from the nursing station. "What is it, babe, are you OK?"

"Please come home. I don't know what I've done. There is blood everywhere."

I excused myself from rounds and rushed home, then sprinted up the stairs to the apartment. The smell of blood greeted me at the front door. I heard her crying, almost wailing, almost sobbing. She sounded profoundly alone. The crying was coming from the bathroom. The bathroom door was closed. I shuddered at the thought of what I would find. I pushed the door open and found her sitting in the bath. The walls and the floor were covered in blood. Her wrists were slit open and the blood flowed into the warm bath water. She was wearing a Mickey

Mouse nightshirt, which was soaked with her blood and her tears. I was heartbroken to see her in so much misery. I realized then that I did not really understand her. The question I had asked myself those months earlier in Johannesburg was still the question I was asking today. What was the mental pain she experienced that only death could alleviate? What caused such torment and such intolerable anguish? I had no answers. Instead, I held her close to me and cried with her. "I am so sorry my baby. I'm so sorry."

I looked at her wrists. The cuts were superficial but numerous. I cleaned her arms and cuts with warm water then bandaged her wrists with gauze. Finally she spoke. "Please promise me that you will never leave me," she begged.

"I promise that I will never leave you," I said, holding her tightly. I helped her back to the bedroom. She was pale and weakened by the loss of blood. Softly I whispered, "Baby, I need to go back to finish rounds. If you want you can come along. Maybe my job won't threaten you as much if you see what I do." She placed her head on my chest and nodded.

"What are you going to tell people when they see the bandages?" she asked.

"We'll tell them that you chaffed them on the pottery wheel while you were molding clay."

Back at the hospital she waited at the nursing station while I finished rounds. After that, we went to the children's ward where I was monitoring the progress of a four-year-old child who had been abandoned by his mother. He had been found close to death and taken to the hospital for treatment. He had developed a condition where his brain fluid could not easily flow through the brain, causing his head to swell to the size of a big pumpkin. His eyes bulged and he quickly tired when he tried to stand because of the weight of his head. However, the child had a beaming smile that had endeared him to all the staff. He was waiting to be flown to Cape Town to have a procedure that would reduce the fluid build-up in his head. Jacqueline took immediate pity on the boy and gave him the box of M&Ms that she had been eating.

As unpredictable as she was, Jacqueline always showed compassion to those whom she perceived to be less fortunate than she was. She never felt threatened by the sick or oppressed, and there were plenty of both in South Africa. In moments when she was with anyone more vulnerable than she herself was, a kind, puerile selflessness would show. "You did great with that little kid. I can't believe that you don't want children," I said. "He reminded me of me. I wish that I could be cared for as much as he is. I AM a baby. I AM a child. Please don't forget that."

I felt exhausted that evening. I wondered what I was doing. I wondered what it was that I was trying to prove. I thought of all the choices that I made every day. Some of those choices, I had made, like smoking cigarettes and marijuana, not exercising, drinking too much, eating too much fat. All led me closer to death. Other choices, like choosing love and honesty over hate and mistrust, had set me free. I felt that I had a choice to make. I could choose to get out of the relationship at that point, but I convinced myself that if I could get through it with her, then she would learn to trust, and I would become a more patient and understanding man.

CHAPTER 19

The compassion that Jacqueline had shown for the ill child gave me an idea. She did so well when she did not feel threatened with abandonment or when there could be no doubt that the love she was receiving was unconditional. I asked her if she wanted a puppy and she glowed at the prospect. She spent the next few days scanning the newspapers. One evening I came home and found what appeared to be the rear end of a large, fluffy, orange rabbit growling under the bed. It darted after some unseen object and then reappeared as a dog a few moments later. Jacqueline laughed at the antics of the puppy, a three-month-old cocker spaniel. The dog had so much energy that he seemed to bounce rather than walk, but when he did walk he wagged his tail with such force, that he appeared to swagger like the bear in the *Jungle Book*. We named him Balu.

Balu quickly became attached to us, particularly to Jacqueline. The presence of the dog seemed to calm her, and for a while her fear of abandonment faded. While I was at the hospital, Jacqueline would take Balu for walks and house-train him. But soon even the puppy was not able to keep her from thinking about her own emptiness. Again she grew restless and found grievance with the smallest frustration. She was becoming more depressed and I felt more pressure to do something to relieve her of her misery. One evening after work she told me that she had an idea. She told me that she wanted me to transfer to a hospital closer to home. The idea appealed to me too, not so much because I was unhappy with my job but more because I felt emotionally depleted. I needed help to deal with Jacqueline's intensity and unpredictability. Back home I was sure that she would once again be able to get herself a job. At least she would have her friends and family to visit with during the hours I was away.

The next morning I woke early and called the teaching hospitals back in Johannesburg but all the intern posts had been filled. Still, the idea of leaving had taken root in Jacqueline's head. She would not tolerate an entire year in the desert. "I guess I could commute back and forth. You know, go home, spend two weeks and then come back for a week," she offered. Once again she was looking for a way to make the relationship work. She suggested a schedule of spending a week with me in Windhoek, alternating with, and before her anticipated frustration with my work schedule set in, a week at home. "I spoke to my grandmother this morning. She told me that she would pay for the tickets."

We agreed to test out her idea and bought her a ticket to go home. Immediately Jacqueline seemed more at ease. The next day, I drove her to the airport and she left for Johannesburg. I had thought that her leaving would be easy for me, but instead I found myself missing her desperately. Her emotional hold on me, and her companionship, were far more profound than I had expected. Without her being with me, I found that my feelings were strangely without context. My joys, sorrows and fears had become subject to Jacqueline's state of mind. I could not generate feelings for their own sake without feeling guilty. Yet she had only just left and I missed her. Tears blurred my vision on the drive back to the apartment. The emotion was more complex than just sadness at her not being with me. There was also a contradictory feeling, a sense of being free and a sense of being able to breathe again. I took pleasure at the thought of calling my family, unencumbered by the possibility of discovery by Jacqueline, then followed by one of her outbursts. But then my fear that she would discover this betrayal, or even that I had thought of it, made me anxious. I pulled over to the side of the road and sat in the car for 10 minutes trying to make sense of these feelings. I couldn't make sense of these feelings, but the 10 minutes had cleared my tears, and I made it home safely.

One evening the charge-nurse paged me to ask about a terminally ill patient. The situation was complex. His family wanted him to come home and did not want him to be on the intravenous morphine that was reducing his pain from cancer. We spent a long time discussing the options. Immediately after I hung up, the phone rang. It was Jacqueline. "Hi, baby," I said excitedly. "What's going on? How are you doing?"
"Who were you speaking to?" she demanded. "As soon as I turn my back, you get on the phone with your family again." It was as if she had read my earlier thoughts. I felt guilty for this and then angry at feeling guilty. "It was the ward. I was doing my work." Quickly she became her some-times-sweet self. "I'm sorry baby, I just miss you terribly. I wanted to talk to you and hear your voice again. I'll be back soon." There was a yearning to her voice that appealed to me. I slept well that night.

A week later I picked her up at the airport. "Babe, you are going to love me so much. I didn't sit around the last two weeks. I went to a hospital in Pretoria. It's only thirty miles from my parents' home. I spoke to the medical director. God, I was good. I totally seduced him! He is going to offer you an internship for your remaining ten months. Isn't that great? They will have a position ready in two weeks. Time to start packing!"

One of the reasons I had chosen Windhoek was because I wanted to work in a community based health-service. I wanted to be in a small hospital, one where I could practice all of medicine from dermatology to obstetrics, not isolating care to one specific organ of the body. This desire to do community medicine in a small town came into direct conflict with Jacqueline's needs. She needed the anonymity of a big city. "God, I don't want the neighbors to know our business and then spread it around. In a town like this everybody will know in days. How do you think that will make me feel?"

I had conflicting priorities and goals, but now she was my family. I didn't want her to be miserable because of something that could so easily be changed. I decided that she was right, so the next day I went to the hospital administration to explain my decision. The medical director said, "We are not surprised. The housing administrator called us when you requested a change in your living quarters. Good luck in Pretoria. I think you'll need it." They seemed to understand, but I am sure that in that small community nothing got missed. Her tantrums had not been quiet.

Jacqueline was happy now, almost euphoric. She had our few belongings packed a week ahead of our departure. For her, my decision to go back to Johannesburg was a new level of commitment. "Babe, thank you so much. No one would ever have done that for me before." She cooked every night, and scrubbed the apartment clean every day, just to keep busy. She went out and bought Cadbury's chocolate, which we ate by the slab-full while we watched videos. "If we could choose to spend the rest of our lives doing this, I would make the choice right now," she said happily. During the next few days, we had neither a fight nor a single cruel word between us. I believed that she was beginning to believe in herself and to hold my love for her inside her mind. I believed that she was healing.

With two days to go before our departure, I told Jacqueline that I was going to call my parents to let them know what we were up to. Jacqueline's mood shifted rapidly. She became suddenly irritable and then just as suddenly calm. After a brief phone call, we went to wash a last load of laundry when my pager went off. I had to return to the ward to evaluate a patient who had made a sudden turn for the worse. Jacqueline started screaming, "What are you doing to me? Just because you think I'm better doesn't mean that you can act as if I'm normal. Just because we're going home doesn't mean that you can call or see your parents whenever you want to." I had to get to the ward. "Don't walk away. Listen to me!" she shrieked. She ran up to me, and then grabbed my pager, throwing it to the floor. It smashed open.

"What the hell are you doing? We are going to have to pay for the thing. You're an idiot." I surprised myself. It was the first time that I had ever insulted her. She picked up a pair of scissors, pointing them at me. I moved to take them away from her.

"Take another step, and I will squeeze your balls so hard that you'll never come again," she threatened. The thought of this made me shudder, but foolishly, I dared her to try. "You wouldn't." With scissors in one hand she moved in quickly, grabbed my groin, and started to squeeze. I grabbed her hand and pulled it away but the damage was done and the pain came quickly. I dropped to the ground. She continued to come after me with the pair of scissors. In a moment of self-preservation, I grabbed a framed oil that she had been working on for her mother and held it up as she lunged. The scissors tore through the canvass easily. She was stunned momentarily as she realized the damage done to her painting. Taking the opportunity of her inaction and still angry with her, I took the scissors and began cutting up the canvass, completely destroying it. She ran at me, but now I was calmer, more aware. I turned and picked her up, carried her to the bedroom and dumped her on the bed. She laughed, which surprised me, and she sat up suddenly and grabbed my shirt, tearing it open. "God that turned me on, I want you to fuck me now!" The anger had turned to desire, but so it was with Jacqueline and that in part was why I loved her. Just like a high-inducing drug, she had a way to make me feel ecstatic, but like the drug there were many lows. I would crash and then need for her to pick me up again.

Later I tried to piece my pager together. The paging mechanism had not been damaged and the case held together well with tape. After returning the pager to the office, I drove slowly back to the apartment. Our time in the desert was done. The car packed, we started the long drive back home as the evening sun bade its farewell in brown, red, orange and blue, and the town settled back for a restful night.

CHAPTER 20

March 1985
Pretoria

The drive home was uneventful. After a long stretch of silence Jacqueline told me that she had lined up a few job interviews for herself, having recognized that she had to have something to do during the day. When I told her I thought that it was a good idea that she get a job, she became angry, saying, "Why is it a good idea? So you can get rid of me? So you don't have to worry about me? Well, let me tell you that if that's the way you feel, maybe I won't go." This time her attempt to rile me was unsuccessful. I didn't respond to her outburst with a no-win answer. Neither, "Yes, so that I can get rid of you," nor, "No, it's because I think that a job will help your self esteem," would have been the right answer. She seemed genuinely happy with my lack of response as we continued on our way.

After a weekend at her parents' house we drove to the Hendrik Verwoerd Hospital in Pretoria. Pretoria, the then capital city of South Africa, lies thirty miles from Johannesburg. At that time, the predominant language spoken in the city and the official language of the hospital was Afrikaans.

Afrikaans is a derivative of Dutch, German and French. It was the language of the white ruling elite and its supporting bureaucracy. I did not speak it well, but well enough to practice basic medicine.

Unlike Katatura Hospital, the Verwoerd Hospital was affiliated with the local medical school and bore all the trademarks of academic establishment, with grand carvings of the great pioneers in medicine adorning its entrance hall. Like Katatura Hospital, the Verwoerd provided some inexpensive and characterless housing. After reviewing the limited choices, we settled on a corner apartment. The next day Jacqueline headed back to her interviews in Johannesburg and I met with the administrative secretary for a schedule of my assignments. The first rotation would be a two-month stint on a pediatric in-patient unit. The call schedule was one night on-call in three. "You won't get any sleep when you are on call," warned the friendly assistant. "The kids are very sick, but the staff knows their stuff. You can trust them." After my first night on-call, I knew that she was right. Katatura had been humane in its call demands, and there had always been time for a few hours of sleep. Now the expectations were clearer, the problems more complex, and the chief residents more demanding. Jacqueline decided to move back to her parents' house for my nights on call. "I can't get any sleep anyway. You get paged too much."

On the days I was on-call, I would get to work by seven in the morning and not get home until six in the evening the next day. When I wasn't on-call, it was a straight 11-hour day. There was no time to exercise, and Jacqueline spent her early evenings after work cooking lavish, butter-filled comfort meals or finding restaurants that would do the same. In the five months that I had known her I had put on close to forty pounds. "You are eating so much because you are miserable," my mother told me one day. "It's a substitute for love." I couldn't think about whether she was right or not. The idea that I was substituting food for love was more than I could handle during the brutality of the work schedule. I looked forward to being with Jacqueline in the evenings and she seemed happy with her new job. She had finally accepted a position at a beauty counter in a large department store. The job worked out well for her because she did not need to be in until after ten in the morning and could leave by three. The schedule gave her a good chance to succeed because she liked to sleep in late in the mornings, and then be at home when I returned from the hospital.

Jacqueline had not been able to keep any of her previous jobs for any significant period of time. She told me that she had had problems with her bosses, with her co-workers or with the work schedule. "I just told them to get fucked, or I didn't show up, and then I told my mother to call them and say that I had quit," she explained.

This cosmetic job was different. Her pay was based mainly on commissions so she did well. There were times when she was so angry that all I could see was the ugliness of her character and I couldn't bear spending time with her. But most of the time this was not the case with Jacqueline. Partly it was because she was beautiful. No other word would do her justice. She was not cute, or gorgeous, or stunning, or dazzling, or elegant. And even when I was angry with her, her beauty overcame me. It did her a disservice in a way because it hid the pain and the fear and the emptiness. In some sense she was like a mirage, an empty promise that teases with hope, but is ultimately barren. But she was beautiful, and so she sold cosmetics magnificently.

A few weeks after the start of my new position, Jacqueline had another idea. "Why is it that I have to drive an hour in heavy traffic to get to work and then drive another hour back to this apartment only to sit around and wait for you? I think that we should move back to my parents' home for the nights that you are not on call and then at least when

I get home, my brothers or my family will be there or I could meet up with a friend. My mother would cook all the meals and she would do the laundry. On the nights that you are on-call you could stay at the apartment here."

"We have to give Pretoria some time. We just got here," I protested feebly. I did not have the will to fight her on this, and some of what she said appealed to me. "Can we agree to talk about it again after we have tried to settle here?" I asked unconvincingly. I was at the point of complete breakdown now. By being with Jacqueline, I had lost control of my emotions and my weight. Now, if we moved back to Johannesburg, I would lose control of my autonomy and, increasingly, or so I felt, of my life. But Jacqueline was getting closer to the shelter of being in a familiar and predictable environment. I felt that it was only a matter of time until the subject of moving to her parents' house came up again. I knew that when that happened I would lose that battle too.

Work was demanding. The first two months were spent on the pediatric surgical floor. I was happy to end the rotation. I was sure that I didn't want to specialize in pediatric surgery after seeing the young children with kidney cancers and blocked bowels. The doctors doing this work were surely answering to a higher calling. I checked my schedule. Obstetrics and Gynecology was next, and I told Jacqueline so one evening. "God, I hope that you wash yourself well before you touch me with those smelly fingers. Aren't you disgusted with yourself, spending your days telling women to spread their legs and looking up their vaginas? Why can't you get a real job like a real man? I am sure that there are plenty of men that appreciate my body. How would you like it if I invited men over and started feeling their balls?" The tension was back, and again it worsened with the demands of my rigorous on-call schedule and nights away from home. For me though, the nights that I was called in were a reprieve. They provided a sleepless calm before the certain storm the next day.

One night my pager went off during supper. A young woman had arrived by ambulance in early labor and some bleeding. "Shit man!" shouted Jacqueline. "There you go again! Why the fuck should I stay here if you are never going to be home?"

"But it's the work that I do," I protested.

"Bullshit, you asshole. It's what you have chosen to do. It is a choice to not be with me. I could be with another man, and maybe that's what you need. A little competition to keep you interested. So many men want me and you know it. Maybe I should be with somebody who works a real job. Somebody who doesn't think that work is more important than me."

Jacqueline reliably resorted to the threat to be with another man whenever she felt that I wasn't paying her enough attention. Predictably, I felt threatened and she knew it. It was her way of making me feel inadequate and it worked. My mother once told me: "If you want your wife to love you, then you have to be a provider and a protector. Even if you love her, without protecting and providing for her and her children, she will never respect you." I had taken this wisdom to heart, but with Jacqueline I felt I was failing in my mission to be a good husband. That sense of failure was intolerable, so I lashed out. "If you do that, I'll leave you," I threatened. "No wonder men have always left you. You make life impossible for them," I said vengefully.

"But you know that about me. You promised me better. You promised never to leave me." I felt guilty for having retaliated. I was caught in the trap of hating her for the very weaknesses that had drawn me to her. But worse, I had promised her that I would love her despite her insecurities and rage. By promising that I would never leave her, I had guaranteed her unconditional love. She continued to put this promise to the test.

"We both knew that this was going to be a difficult year," I said defensively. "Damn you. What about me? Who is going to take care of me?" she cried.

"I am your husband, not your therapist. And I do take care of you. I spend every waking second that I am not at the hospital with you."

I turned to look for my white coat, and then heard a loud pathetic scream, almost a screech, behind me. I turned to face her and she lashed out, striking me in the face. I covered my face while she continued her attack, kicking and hitting. Finally I grabbed her arms and held her in a bear hug. She continued to scream, "Help, heeeelp, he's trying to kill me." Foolishly, I tried to put my hand across her mouth, but she bit hard into my palm. I heard the neighbors at the door and eventually the landlord opened the door.

"Please," I asked, "Call an ambulance. My wife isn't well." They didn't appeared convinced, so I let her go. "You fucking call an ambulance and I'll kill myself now, I swear it," she threatened, grabbing a kitchen knife. Someone asked me if they should call the police but I assured them that we had gone through this before and that I could handle it. My pager went off. "Dr. Walker, you are needed in the delivery room right away!"

"OK darling, we won't call an ambulance, but I have to get to the delivery room. I want you to relax, watch TV, and I'll be back as soon as I'm done." One of the neighbors, a nurse, offered to spend the evening with Jacqueline.

"I just can't take it anymore," said Jacqueline. She started to cry and put the knife down. "Go, I'm just going to sleep tonight."

The next morning she woke me early and we lay in bed, talking. "Babe, I know that we just moved here from Windhoek, but even being this close to Johannesburg isn't helping. I just can't take it being here all alone with nothing to do. I just go crazy looking at the walls." Jacqueline had arranged her schedule so that she would start work in the late morning and be done by early afternoon. The rest of the time she chose to spend at the apartment, so she felt isolated. "What would help? You could read, watch TV, or paint or get a full-time job or do some housework. Your mom said that I should get you to do housework."

"If only we could live at my parents' house. You promised that we would talk about it again, remember? If only we could leave Pretoria, everything would be perfect. I could talk to my mom and my friends when you're away and I promise you I would look to get a full-time job. You could still keep the apartment for whenever you are on call. At least I wouldn't get so lonely. It drives me crazy. I'm sorry for what I did last night." She smiled warmly. "I love you so much, you're so good to me. I know that things will work out."

"OK, if you find yourself a full-time job, I'll agree to move back. But you must find a job." Jacqueline increased her work schedule from four hours to six hours a day, and I kept my end of the deal and agreed to make her parents' house our base. I resigned myself to the thirty-mile commute to work every day.

Even though I had spoken to my parents periodically since my marriage to Jacqueline, I had not seen them in more than four months. But now Jacqueline seemed increasingly more convinced that I would not abandon her. One morning I suggested having lunch with my parents. At first she appeared irritated with the idea, but later that evening, after a session with her therapist, she agreed to the plan without further fuss. I was heartened by her reaction. She so hated how close I was to my family, so I felt that she was giving something back to me. What had bothered me most about not seeing them was not the absence of seeing them only; but that I had become terrified of even suggesting it to Jacqueline for fear that she would erupt in anger. Her agreeing to meet with my parents was a breakthrough. She agreed to lunch as long as it was on neutral ground. We settled on a restaurant at a nearby country club.

As the weekend approached, Jacqueline became more irritable and demanding. I did everything I could to make sure that things would work out. On Thursday she said, "Look, I don't want to go. They are your parents. You go. You haven't seen them in a long time." I recognized the trap immediately.

"Darling, you know that I want you to be there with me. You are doing so well. I want you to be there for them to see how happy you make me. You are my wife." She seemed appeased by my words and I hoped she would believe and hold on to them for at least the next two days. If Jacqueline could now believe that I could care for her at the same time that I could care for another, or that by caring for somebody else it was not taking away from my care for her, then she had truly made progress.

I had ordered my parents to be on their best behavior, and they reassured me that this was to be a dinner of conciliation. They promised that it would be the first step on the return to normality. I was happy, but it seemed to me that happiness was no longer an emotion that I could feel for its own sake. I had to justify everything to myself. "I am happy because…I am sad because…I am angry because…" The natural ebb and flow of feeling from within, and without apparent cause, was gone. Sometimes when I felt happy, I felt guilty for feeling what Jacqueline felt so rarely.

My father called that Saturday morning to say that the country club required a coat and tie. I wanted my father to know that I appreciated the effort that he was making, so I chose a tie that he had given me some time back.

"What's that?" asked Jacqueline, pointing to the tie. I tensed, anxious, wary of her question.

"It's a tie. My dad gave it to me once."

"Well, take it off, it's ugly."

I had to hold firm. "Come on Jacqueline, it's a peace offering. I'm going to wear it. It's no big deal. Why don't you just get ready and we'll go? They're waiting for us."

"You just can't let go of them, can you?" Her voice was rising.

"Listen, this is your parents' house that we're living in. I haven't seen mine in months. I am not the one who can't let go."

"Yes, but I need them. I need to see them and feel them and be near them. God, I know that you know that. I know what you are trying to do to me. Don't compare my situation to yours."

"OK, let's just relax and go," I said softly.

"Take that fucking tie off!" she demanded.

"This tie is not an issue. Let's go."

"The tie is ugly and it shows your father's bad taste."

I turned to the mirror one last time in order to straighten the tie out. "Here let me help you with it," she said. I turned, confused, as she grabbed the tie and with the slice of a pair of scissors, cut it in half. "Now you can take it off. That should make it easier," she said calmly. "Let's go. You can borrow one of my dad's."

A sense of utter disbelief and rage and violation overwhelmed me. I sat on the bed with clenched fists, and cried for the loss of the tie. I wanted her to feel the hurt that I felt, but even worse, at that moment I wanted to be the one hurting her. The thought of hurting her was sobering. "She is sick, she is sick, she is sick…" I repeated over and over. I swallowed, as if by doing so, I could move the anger to the pit of my stomach. Eventually I stood up. "OK, let's go now."

"I am not ready yet," she said.

"Bye, I'm leaving."

Her parents had heard the commotion and were hovering outside the bedroom. They saw the anger in my face as I left the room. "What happened?" I threw down the cut tie and headed for the car. Jacqueline came running after me. I slammed the car door shut. "OK, OK but give me just a minute," she insisted. She tapped on the car window, lips offering a conciliatory kiss. I lowered the window and she leant into the car to kiss me. "Sorry, sorry, sorry." Immediately she grabbed the keys out of the ignition. "I told you to wait until I was ready. Are you fucking deaf? You weren't going to leave without me, were you?" She headed for the house, and I ran after her. He mother stopped me and handed me her car keys. "Here take my car. Just go."

I got into the car and left. Free at last. I headed for the gate. Behind me, I heard the unmistakable sound of the Ford Mustang revving. Jacqueline's mother's car was a slow, low-powered excuse of a car. Quickly Jacqueline caught up to me and overtook me. I cringed at the thought of the action on the narrow, suburban, potentially child-filled street. Suddenly she braked, and I swerved off the road to avoid hitting her. I drove around her, as she had stalled, but again she caught up and I turned down another street to get away. Her mother's car was no match, and it was crazy driving around like this. Defeated, I returned to the house. We were already an hour late for lunch; meanwhile she decided to continue driving around the block. Faster and faster and faster she drove, but even worse, in a low gear. The sound was the terrifying grind of an over-revved engine. Her parents stood there watching, feeling as hopeless and lost as I was. I prayed that a child wouldn't run out. I heard a crash and then more screeching.

Jacqueline's brother called to me. "Your mother is on the phone." I told her of the nightmare. She said that she understood and that she wanted to pray for us, but I felt too empty for prayers. I heard my car coming down the driveway. There was a dent in the front fender. Jacqueline looked exhausted. "I crashed into a rock," she admitted.

It was at this moment that I realized that I might not be able to keep my promise to be with her for the rest of my life. Previously, the thought had crossed my mind, but had left quickly.

I had been committed to the belief that my love for her would cure her. Now I looked at her, as miserable as she was, and I could not conjure up this thought anymore. I believed that giving her what she had never had; - strong, unrelenting, and unconditional love - would fill the emptiness and uncertainties she felt. It was never enough. How much would she test me? "No one could ever love me forever," she had said so many times. Maybe she would prove this to be right. She kept upping her demands on me, slowly destroying whatever hope there was to show her that she was lovable. I wasn't sure that I could keep with her unrelenting neediness.

Was it so terrifying to be loved, or was the thought of losing such love even more terrifying? I didn't know what the answer was, and I seriously doubted that I would ever find out. I was empty and could no longer feel, so I had nothing to give.

I couldn't understand it. Short of transplanting myself into her body, what would it ever take for her to hold me inside of her? She told me that she felt the feeling when we made love, but that the further I moved away from her the duller the feeling became. I felt that I had given everything that I could, and the paradox became clear to me then. The more I gave, the more she wanted, because I could never quite give enough. There was always that little bit more. In order to give more, I would have to be strong. Yet the more I gave, the more pathetic and weak I became. It could never work.

Chapter 21

Suburban Johannesburg
May 1985

Jacqueline was uncharacteristically subdued after the car scene. She poured her remaining energy into her work at the cosmetics counter. We moved quietly through the days, not mentioning the event, as if not talking about it would make it disappear, make it never having existed. It would be her birthday in six weeks and I wanted to make it a memorable day.

Jacqueline could not believe that people loved her, or at least she found it hard to believe it when they were not physically with her, reassuring her of the fact. Without the person being in her presence, any feeling of the permanence of love seemed to disappear. It seemed normal to me to be thinking about her a lot of the time. Planning for her birthday was an act of love, not an unusual act of love, but one that goes unseen. Thinking about where we would go and what we would do was not like a dozen roses which she could hold, and smell, but it was thinking about her and what would make her happy. Increasingly I realized that these unseen acts of love meant nothing to her. She could not internalize them, because they weren't tangible. It was as if they had never happened.

However, had I not planned for her birthday, or had I forgotten it altogether, she would have seen this as proof that I didn't love her.

On the day of her birthday I left the hospital early, and stopped to pick up a bunch of peonies. As I got back in the car, my voice-activated beeper went off. "Dr. Walker, call Ward Three immediately." The voice sounded urgent, and I stopped at a pay phone. The charge nurse answered, "Mr. Smith, in bed six, has had a sudden rise in temperature. He has a fever of 104. He looks terrible." A sudden dread fell over me. I hated Mr. Smith. He was doing this on purpose. Surely I would arrive late for Jacqueline, and she would believe that I had done it on purpose. "You don't love me more than anything," she would say. But Mr. Smith was dying. I certainly had to take care of him.

I drove back quickly. A fellow intern was still at the hospital. She told me that she was on-call that night, and that I should order all the tests that I wanted. She would take over the case after that and review the results. I checked to see that Mr. Smith was comfortable, and not in any clear emergency. I ordered some X-Rays and blood work. Some Tylenol and a cool glass of water lowered his temperature. I reassured him that he would be OK and that I was leaving him in the good hands of my colleague. He smiled back at me through thin lips. "Thank you."

I drove back home, too fast, but I was already late. I thought of the past six weeks and reminded myself that she had done well. Moreover, there was nothing I could do. I was in peak-hour traffic.

I arrived home at six fifteen. Jacqueline was waiting in the driveway. "Where the fuck have you been?" she demanded, grabbing the peonies out of my hands, and throwing them angrily to the floor.
"If you flip out, you can forget about tonight," I threatened. She screamed loud and long and came toward me. I thought of the scissors

that she had previously used on my tie, and made the decision to run around the back of the house, heading for the pool. She ran back into the house and her mother tried to console her. "He's back. I told you he'd be back. You married a doctor. Just go out and have a nice dinner." "He could have tried harder," she cried. "He could have tried harder." She came out again, "Anthony, come here!"

"Not until you calm down." She went back into the house and picked up a potted plant, then hurled it at the living-room wall. She picked up another and threw it through a small window, then another one at the Chagall-like flower arrangement that she had painted for me. She sat down and sobbed inconsolably into her hands. "He could have tried harder." I came to her and put my arm around her shoulders. She buried her face in my neck, and her body relaxed. Finally the anger had gone, and we were able to enjoy an Italian meal without further incident.

I had a nightmare that night. Jacqueline's mother was teaching a cooking class. A pot on the stove had started to boil over. She wasn't strong enough to hold the lid down and asked me to take over. I held it down as tightly as I could, but eventually could hold it no longer. The pot erupted and I got scalded. She thanked me for holding the lid, but the water had spilled over, so she would have to add more water. She asked me to hold the lid down again.

CHAPTER 22

Early on in the relationship, Jacqueline had asked me to promise her that I would never hit her. It seemed a strange request, but she told me that all of her previous boyfriends had hit her at some point in their relationship with her. I could never imagine myself hitting her, or anyone else for that matter. I promised her that I would never hit her.

Our relationship was physical though, in love and in anger. When Jacqueline was angry she threw, punched, bit, scratched, and kicked. In turn I would dodge, block, and run. Occasionally, I would wrestle with her to hold her. Her arms would flail as she attempted to scratch me. Once I held her, so she yelled. The time I tried to put my hand across her mouth she simply bit it. I ended up with stitches and a tetanus booster.

One evening I arrived home and headed straight for bed, then quickly fell asleep. The previous night I had had no sleep after being on-call. I felt Jacqueline shaking me. "I told you never to bring your work home. When you get home your time is my time." Too tired to argue, I fell back asleep. "Get the fuck up!!!" she shrieked. I jumped up with frazzled nerves. In her hand she had a pair of scissors. "This should wake you up!" I fell back on the bed and grabbed her hand. And then I slapped her.

Jacqueline stopped, stunned. "You promised me." She held her hand to her face. I was awake then. "I'm sorry, I'm sorry, I'm sorry," I held her. "I promise you that I will never do that again." For the briefest of moments it had felt good to hurt her, and then instantly everything was wrong. I started to cry. I had lost complete control of everything I believed in. I felt nauseous.

"You promised."

"I'm sorry."

"I can never trust you again. I can never believe your promises. You aren't any better than any of the others. My mother was wrong. You aren't my guardian angel." She looked at her face in the mirror. Her cheek was red and swollen, the pain magnified by her tears. Her face had drawn me to her. My promise of enduring love and care had drawn her to me. Both were now damaged, though her face would heal quicker. She used make-up to hide the mark on her face. At home she trailed me like a chastened puppy. I was angry at my loss of control. It took another month before she argued with me again; it was an eerie and uncomfortable time.

CHAPTER 23

Jacqueline saw her therapist every other week. They would spend the hour and a half working on strategies to control her rage. "I am all these pieces all at once," Jacqueline once told me, "and I can't hold them all together. I keep falling apart. Don't you see why it would be better for me to be dead than to live this way? I wish that you could be inside me to hold me together. That's why I get so frightened when you leave me."

I was finding it increasingly difficult to have the strength necessary to deal with her unpredictable moods and raging behavior. At one point, her therapist referred her to a psychiatrist. "In America, they are trying antipsychotics and mood-stabilizers for this condition. I haven't had much luck with these medications, but we can try," he told her. Jacqueline agreed. First, she took Mellaril, which the psychiatrist said would help her think more clearly. "It hasn't done anything for my thinking. Obviously because there is nothing wrong with my thinking, but it helps me sleep better." She also tried Tegretol to control her moods, but she felt that it didn't work so she stopped taking it. She took a dose of Valium once, but it made her feel more rageful. "God, I never want to feel like that again," she said, after she had calmed down some hours later.

Intellectually I felt that I understood her illness better, but I had a hard time separating what was illness from what sometimes looked like willful vengeance. She blamed everything that went wrong on her condition. Maybe I could have understood this better, but I was her husband and not her therapist. I had a hard time remembering that sometimes. The course of my every day was set by her moods. I had no control over this. If she was happy, I felt calm. When she was angry, I was edgy all day, unable to focus at work. I wondered if this chaos was what she felt inside. It was unbearable for both of us. I was beginning to understand her, but it was draining me. The more I gave of myself, the more she expected me to give. It was as if each time she would set a higher standard for my capacity to give of myself. Yet there was no end point, because it was never good enough. She felt that I could always give more. I felt that I could never show her enough love without her doing something even more destructive to prove to me that she was unlovable.

After we had returned from Windhoek, and we were back in Johannesburg, I tried to reconnect with some of my old classmates. They returned the calls, but Jacqueline never gave me the messages. "I wonder why they aren't calling back?" I asked her.
"Don't worry babe. You don't need them. You've got me."

Once Howard called, and I answered.
"Hey brother, I've been trying to get hold of you for the last few months. I guess you're a busy man, even too busy for your friends," he laughed.
"What are you talking about? I had no idea."
"Didn't Jacqueline tell you I had called?"
"No, she said nothing." Later I confronted her on this. "Why didn't you tell me that Howard had called?"
She erupted into rage. "What the fuck do you need any of your friends for now? You've got me. What do you want to talk to them about that you can't say to me? Soon you'll want to go out for a drink with them

and leave me here by myself, but I tell you the minute you try that, I'll be fucking another man." There was no middle ground for her. It was always all or nothing. Later that week I called Howard from the hospital and we agreed to a secret meeting for lunch at the hospital cafeteria. My stomach pitted with anxiety, fearing that she would find out. When she was in one of her moments of madness, there was nothing to do. I realized that trying to talk to her or "do something" did little to calm the rage. In the big picture just my being there helped her more than anything else. I didn't know how to get out of the moments. They sucked me in each time and then spat me out. Each time I had less confidence in myself.

Howard drove up from Johannesburg. His internship, like mine, was half complete. Unlike mine, he had spent the entire time at one hospital, the Johannesburg General. "God, Howard, in the last six months I have worked in two hospitals, while living in three cities in two countries."
"You're not yourself. You've lost your spark," he consoled me. "I wish we'd understood more about Borderlines last year. She didn't look that bad. You were thinking with the wrong head." I laughed with him, but the laughter brought me no joy.
"Thanks for coming. I wish I could see you all the time, but she feels so threatened by anyone I get close to."
"There is a Jewish teaching that goes like this: The way of the righteous and men of good deeds is to love peace and take pleasure in the welfare of their fellow-man and draw them closer to the Torah. They would not wantonly destroy even a mustard seed. They are grieved and oppressed at the sight of waste and destruction. If they could save anything from being destroyed they would do so with all their power." He paused, and then added, "You are a good man. You'll find the way. Call me whenever you want to," he offered. Then he continued with mischievous eyes, "Remember, you promised me that you were going to go into psychiatry to help children. If you're not careful, the only psychiatry you'll be seeing will be on my therapy couch."

CHAPTER 24

Jacqueline and I had been together for six months. One morning I woke up feeling more miserable than usual. My clothes did not fit well. The bathroom scale read two hundred and twenty pounds. I stood in front of the mirror and looked at the roll of fat that hung over my pants. "You're hideous," I told the reflection. I felt both lonely and alone. Everything annoyed me. During hospital rounds I compared my misery to the suffering of the patients I was treating. I felt that I needed to do that in order not to feel so badly.

If we were going to stay together I had to change my role in the relationship. I felt that it had to be more on my terms. I had given up my life to prove my love to her. But it seemed to me that all my efforts had not been enough to make her feel more secure. I had to begin to distance myself from Jacqueline and become stronger. My mood could not be dependent on how her day was going. I had to stop shying away from her aggression. I felt that her support systems, her family, her therapist, and her friends enabled her dysfunction. This was not deliberate, but they provided her an outlet for her rage without forcing her to face her fears. They didn't challenge her to change because, like me, they treated her delicately for fear of unleashing the monster.

I had to move her away from these supports. I had to force her to realize that she could survive without them. With this new sense of conviction, I made the decision to apply for a residency post in the States. I was certain that leaving South Africa had to be the first step in restoring control of my life, and of providing Jacqueline with any hope of breaking the despair that her life was.

I was finally beginning to face the reality of my situation. It seemed ironic that I wanted to go to the land whose movies had so appealed to, and influenced, my sense of romanticism and adventure that I created my very own *Fatal Attraction*.

I was determined to study psychiatry and I knew that I would get no better training than in America. It was at this time that my deceit began. I sent for applications to nine different residency programs and used my father's home as the return address. After the packages had arrived, my father paged me at the hospital. I picked them up at his house, and took them to the hospital where I left them in a locker, for fear that Jacqueline would discover them at the apartment. One weekend my on-call duty began that Saturday morning and ended the next Sunday at noon. Jacqueline spent the weekend in Johannesburg. After uneventful Saturday morning rounds, I retrieved the applications from the locker. I sat down at the nurses' station, and opened the first package.

Make sure to complete all sections as any omissions may lead to delays in processing your application. Please return the following with your 12-page application:

1. A letter from the office of the dean
2. Three letters of recommendation from supervisors
3. A transcript of your medical school grades
4. A resume

5. Four passport-size photos with your signature on the back
6. A half page essay telling us why you want to come to our training program
7. A cashier's check for $120 (processing fee—do not send cash, or foreign currency)

The list continued. I feared that the chance of discovery with all the application requirements was great. I wondered how I would get away in order to have the passport photographs taken. My father told me that he would take care of the cashier's checks. I could not risk having any mail inadvertently sent to our Pretoria apartment or to Jacqueline's parents' house in Johannesburg.

When I reviewed all the packages, I found that much of the requisite paperwork was similar for all the applications. That meant just one trip to the photographer, one call to the dean's office, and one call to each of three supervisors. Again I used my parents' home as a return address and their phone number as contact number. Over the next few weeks, I completed the applications, a page at time, during breaks at work. By then, the letters and transcripts had arrived. Again I lied to Jacqueline, and told her that my new rotation started half an hour early. I used the extra time to meet with my father at the hospital and gave him the completed packages, which he then mailed off. Six weeks later, all the applications had been sent.

Those days with Jacqueline were good. I did little to antagonize her, or at least she did not seem to be as easily bothered by the things I did. Perhaps I was extra sensitive to the fear of her discovering my subterfuge. Perhaps unconsciously I had already given up on her and did not feel that I had to challenge her any longer. In any case Jacqueline was happy, and she was doing well at work, a job that she had held for far longer than any other that she had ever done. She seemed to be doing better in herself. She laughed more easily, and even made jokes, which was something new for her. One evening we went out for dinner at a Portuguese restaurant. While waiting for our clams stewed in beer, an irate customer at the next table was shouting at the waitress that he had been waiting for his draught beer for some time. "If he wants a draft, why doesn't he shut up and go sit by that open window," Jacqueline quipped. I laughed, not only for the joke, but also for how unexpected it was coming from her.

Her happiness, though, had come at the expense of my own pathetic existence. But seeing her this happy made me not feel as sorry for myself as I had been feeling. To my surprise one afternoon I arrived home to see her in a new jogging outfit. "It's Kappa. So are the running shoes. If we are going to go jogging, at least we should do it in style. You know me. I think that we should jog every day. We could both use it."

Early on in our relationship, Jacqueline's unpredictability had been charming, with her intensity in her search for her identity, her sponta-neous and unconventional lovemaking, and her energy in creating art. But this did not last long and increasingly the only unpredictability was just when the next tantrum would occur. Her sudden decision to go jogging was unexpected and refreshing.
"I agree. What made you think of it?"
"I know how much you like to run. Anyway, I read in my *Cosmo* that running at least thirty minutes four times a week means that you increase your metabolism by burning off an extra 2000 calories. We could both use that. My mother said that she would come too."
"Jacqueline, you're doing great. You're joking around, you want to start exercising, you seem so much happier. What is it?"
"You're just not provoking me like you used to. Also you don't talk about your parents so much. Maybe we'll even be able to visit them soon," she said, as if she were granting me a favor.

A few weeks later my father called me. I had received responses to my applications. All were positive. All had appointment dates and interviews set up. I was living two lives, but in my secret I had regained some control. I felt sad for Jacqueline, knowing that I would have to tell her soon, knowing the disappointment and betrayal that she would feel. But the worst was knowing that the abandonment that she had predicted, that is, my abandonment of her, would come at a time when her belief in herself was apparently just starting to take root. "In the end, everybody leaves me."

CHAPTER 25

Nearly three months went by without a major incident. There was no throwing, hitting, biting, rage attacks, or suicide threats. One weekend her parents left for vacation, and like adolescents we took over the house and organized a party for each night.

Friday night started with far too much Merlot, and continued with total loss of inhibitions. We danced naked in the pool and fumbled in love in the kitchen. Eventually exhaustion set in, and we fell asleep at some late hour. Some time after that the ringing in my head started I got up for a drink of water, and went back to bed. The ringing started again, and then stopped. It started again. It took a while for me to realize that it wasn't coming from my head. The telephone persisted. "Leave it," muttered Jacqueline. It rang again. Now it began to scare me the way a late night call does.

"Hello?"

"Anthony, it's your bother Michael."

"Hey, what's up? Do you know what time it is?"

"Anthony, I have terrible news. Ryan called. Rachel has just been killed in a car accident."

"What are you talking about?"

"Ryan was driving behind them. He saw everything. He said that Rachel was sitting on the passenger side of the car in front of him. She was on the way back home after being at church with her friends. Some drunken guy drove through a stop sign and into her side of the car. She died instantly."

I hung up and felt cold. I loved my sister, but I had rarely told her how much she meant to me. I had never been a good older brother, often outwardly dismissive of her achievements. In truth I secretly admired her successes. She was the first in the family to graduate with a college degree, the first to own her own car, the first to pay off her college loans, the first to become financially independent of my parents. We teased and ribbed her, but she smiled, and when I needed a summer job, she offered me hers. "I've got connections, I'll just get another." She was self-less. She had been killed by the selfishness of a man who drank and then drove. He too had been killed in the accident. But even in his death I hated him for having taken her.

"My sister just died in a car accident."

It took moments of tragedy to bring out the sympathy that Jacqueline was capable of feeling and showing. I remembered how she had cared for the little boy with the enlarged brain in the hospital in Windhoek. Now she put her arm around me and said simply, "Babe, I'm sorry." I cried and continued to cry, and at some point fell back asleep.

During my time with Jacqueline, I had spent little time with my parents, but I had spent even less time with Rachel. Because of this, to Jacqueline, Rachel was the least threatening of my family members. They had met on two occasions. The first time was soon after Jacqueline and I had started dating. Rachel was preparing to move to Cape Town for college, so the meeting was brief. The second time that she met

Jacqueline was when Rachel came up to Johannesburg during a school vacation to have lunch with us. It was also the last time I would ever see Rachel or speak to her. She told me that she had decided to get a Masters in Psychology. I remember being impressed by how once again Rachel had a clear vision of her life-course.

Always kind, always gentle, and always generous, Rachel told me after lunch, "Anthony, that is what is so great about you. You give hope to people who are miserable. Mom told me about Jacqueline. She seems so happy. If anybody can help her, you can." And that was it; she saw the good in people all the time. My brother Ryan, who had been with her when she died, told me that she prayed for me daily that God would give me the strength to help Jacqueline.

Early the next morning I woke from the nightmare, although I have never experienced such a vivid nightmare. Michael's voice had seemed real. Had he called? "Hi, Mom," I called my mother. She was crying. I remember somebody once telling me that a child who loses a parent is called an orphan but that there is no word for a parent who loses a child. It is unnatural. I could not imagine how much my mother was hurting. Rachel was her first daughter.

Some days after Rachel's death, my mother told me that Rachel's spirit had visited her in the form of a songbird. The bird had told my mother that she was happy to have finally made it to heaven.

My father made the funeral arrangements. In a moment of sudden, raw bitterness towards Jacqueline, I wanted her to try to stop me from going to the funeral by having one of her tantrums. I wanted to get angry at her and yell at her for her insensitivity, and for having kept me from my family. Jacqueline never gave me the opportunity: all throughout the time she was kind and solemn. The hurt did not come from Jacqueline, but from her mother. "Your poor mother," she said. "But at least it's not as bad as losing your only daughter. At least she has two others. That's why some people have a lot of children." I lost total respect for Jacqueline's mother after she made that admission. I felt that this lack of caring had, in part, made Jacqueline the person she was. How could Jacqueline ever believe that anybody cared for her when her mother was so incapable of understanding the loss of a child? How could she not understand the uniqueness of every child's relationship with its parents?

Jacqueline and I flew down to Cape Town for the funeral. Rachel was buried on a mountainside in the wine country of Stellenbosch. After the burial, our collective grief brought us together for some time. Jacqueline's parents and mine were civil to each other. For a while, Jacqueline showed no anger when I suggested that we visit my parents. It struck me that it had taken the loss of my sister's life for Jacqueline to agree to spend time with my family. I wondered how many more lives would be destroyed or lost before my life with Jacqueline became truly normal.

Chapter 26

"Being with your Dad at your sister's funeral made me think about what a hypocrite he is," said Jacqueline on an otherwise relaxed evening, over dinner.

"Why do you say that?" I asked.

"He claims to be such a Christian. At Rachel's funeral he made that speech about love, and how Rachel was pure love. He said that she never judged anybody and treated everybody with kindness. He quoted the song that said, "They will know we are Christians by our love." Nobody would know that he was a Christian using that logic. You see the way he despises me. The way he makes me feel so useless and insignificant. Where is the love there?"

I wasn't sure how to respond to her charge. I knew that it was not so much that my father despised her as much as that he felt that my being with her had put an abrupt halt to my career and personal growth. Because of this, he saw her as playing a very significant role in my life, while at the same time being a person of little consequence to him. He was angry with me for having made the choice that I did, but by disregarding Jacqueline's existence he had made an enemy who would not easily go away. He would have to deal with her whether he liked to or not.

"And do you want to know what else I think about hypocrisy?" she asked further.

"What's that?" I asked.

"I think that everybody is a hypocrite. They all go about pretending that they are better than everybody else. You know me. I say exactly what I mean. Sometimes it's not that pleasant, but it's always true. I don't mince my words. I spit them out with a vengeance. People can't take that. And maybe I am a hypocrite sometimes, but you know what? I accept that. I know that there are contradictions in the way that I act and the things that I say. The worst hypocrisy is not to recognize that you are a hypocrite."

"You're right I guess, but just saying that you are a hypocrite doesn't excuse bad behavior."

"I wasn't saying that it did," she countered, "but on the other hand, people know that I have Borderline Personality Disorder. Your father knows it. You think that it is easy being me? I spend every day thinking whether I should continue trying, or kill myself instead. And it's because I can't take being who I am. It's because I can't stand that I make other people's lives so miserable. Do you think that your father could live by his own Christian values and show some understanding?"

Jacqueline's reflection had been clear and well reasoned. There had been little anger in her deliberation. I agreed with her, yet at the same time I understood that my father's opinion of her came not from a judgment of her character alone, but from his perceived sense that he had lost a son. In either case, the distinction was meaningless for Jacqueline. His attitude towards her was the same either way, and for this she hated him.

CHAPTER 27

I was assigned to spend the final two months of my internship in a surgery rotation. On the first day, the senior resident told me that the rotation would require my being on-call overnight every third night, as well as doing rounds every Saturday and Sunday morning. Moreover, we had to be available to answer any questions on our post-surgery patients, even on our days off, in case the covering doctors had any questions. The requirement was to be within beeper range twenty-four hours per day. As beeper range was only 10 miles, there was no way to live at her parents' home. I realized my luck. It was consistent with my plan to move Jacqueline further away from her support systems.

Hesitantly, I told Jacqueline of the new schedule. "You fucking miserable shit, you're disgusting," she screamed. "Why can't you get a job where you aren't sticking your fingers up vaginas and up shitholes? Do you think that I'm attracted to that? If I had known what you do I would never have married you."

"Where are my keys?" I asked calmly.

"What, are you going to drive away again?" Her parents, hearing the commotion, appeared at the bedroom door. "You see what he is doing? He's trying to drive me crazy. He doesn't care."

"Where are my keys?"

"You want your fucking keys?" she growled, "You want your fucking keys?" she screamed again. "Well, here they are." She had the keys hidden in her coat pocket. She took them out and ran at me, keys clenched in her fist. The ignition key was sticking out like a small knife. She brought it down towards my face cutting into my eyelid. I jumped back, and my vision suddenly dimmed. Blood poured from the cut. Jacqueline dropped the keys and ran, crying, to her room. I grabbed a sweatshirt from the floor to cover my eye, picked up the keys and drove to my parents' house.

"Anthony, what happened? What did she do to you?" asked my mother. "I don't know anymore Mom. This whole thing is too big for me. I just can't do it anymore." The phone rang. "Don't tell her I'm here," I begged.
"It's one of your friends. It's a man," said my younger sister.
"Hello?"
"Hi. I knew you wouldn't answer, so I got my brother to call," said Jacqueline, always calculating. "I just wanted to talk to you. I'm so sorry, you really are the best thing that ever happened to me. I'm so scared that you will leave me that I lose control. Please just come back. I love you so much. I'm sorry."

CHAPTER 28

Late October 1985

The moment after she had stabbed me with the key, I realized that I had been misguided in my belief that I could help her. She had always had a way of appealing to my sense that I could do something. She knew that and manipulated that. I too had manipulated her. I needed somebody to need, although not as much as she did. Emotionally I was tapped out. I ate for comfort; I was fatter but no less empty. My sense of self and purpose had all but disappeared. Most disappointing was coming to terms with the fact that love, after all, could not in and of itself cure all the hurt in the world. Now, the increasing certainty that I would leave Jacqueline, who was so rooted in her own self-destruction, was liberating. If she wanted to follow me to the other side of the world, it would be knowing that this time there would be no turning back. There would be no familiarity to fall back on. If she decided to make the choice to follow me, it would be her last chance to make it with me.

The next morning I woke early, ready for the new rotation. I had bought an intern's guide-to-surgery handbook, but I couldn't find it that morning. I rushed out and stopped briefly at my parents' house. "I know that it seems that it's taken me a long time to figure it out, but I know that I have to leave Jacqueline, or at least I have to leave South Africa and the security that it brings her. Unless there's a miracle, I doubt that she'll be able to make it away from her family. Dad, I know how you feel about Jacqueline, but I do deeply care about her. In those moments when we are having fun, it is the most fun that I have ever had. In those moments when she shows her caring side, she is the most caring person I know. It's unfair of you to think badly of her because of the choices that I have made. I made this mess, but I am going to get out of it." My father tried hard to not show his joy, but immediately he offered me help. "I'll buy the ticket for you, I'll take care of everything," he said excitedly. My mother shook her head. "Sometimes you can be so insensitive," she berated my father, then added, "Anthony, whatever you choose to do, just know that we love you. We will all get through this together."

The South African academic year follows the calendar year (summer falls at the end of the year in the southern hemisphere), so I would have six months of free time before my residency started in June in America. At the time that I had sent off my applications for residency, I had also written a letter to a hospital in England looking for a part-time position. I wanted to take a break before starting my psychiatry training. The hospital in London responded that they had a position available. I now had the airplane tickets, a part-time job and a residency. Almost all the pieces were in place, but the biggest challenge lay ahead.

CHAPTER 29

Early November 1985

The idea of telling Jacqueline that I was ready to leave South Africa terrified me. I became paranoid that she could read my thoughts and that she would discover the secret preparations that I had planned behind her back. I was afraid of what she would do. She was lethal with a knife, for instance. Even a plain set of keys had been damaging. I was afraid to lie in bed with her. I was afraid to get into my car, fearing that she might have tampered with the breaks. I was afraid for my parents. I had the fantasy of going to the airport, my bags packed, and calling her from there, "Hi baby. I'm at the airport. I'm leaving. Bye!" Ultimately, it was clear that I simply had to tell her.

More than just wanting to leave Jacqueline, I wanted to leave the misery that my life had become. I had to take back control of my own sense of self, without allowing her to define my identity. Looking back, I realized that Rachel's death had contributed to this decision. Her life, ended so young at twenty-two, had been more complete and full than my own. She had set her own course and followed it to the end. She had understood the need to control her own life, years before I understood it, but then again she had always been ahead of the boys. Leaving South Africa was not only just about what I wanted; I also held on to the belief that Jacqueline's life could be better than it was. I wanted for her to leave the family and friends that sheltered her from having to deal with her own madness. But this wish for her was independent of my decision to leave South Africa. I would leave with or without her.

I still worried over the timing of telling her. There were eight weeks to go to the end of my internship. It was far too early.

Jacqueline's parents and I had a relationship based on need. I needed them to take care of her when she was angry with me, and they needed me to take care of her when she was angry with them. It was an unstated understanding, but they needed me more. I could always leave Jacqueline, but she would always be their daughter. Because of this, they tried as best they could to make my life as comfortable as possible. Increasingly, I had become suspicious of their every act of support and kindness. I felt that they would do anything to keep me with Jacqueline. I had always been able to talk to both of her parents, but Jacqueline's mother called the shots in the family. I decided to talk to them first. They had their own interests to care for. Together we would come up with a solution.

When I played out the scenarios in my head, I realized that I wasn't telling Jacqueline that I was leaving her. I was offering her a choice, although a choice that I knew would be very hard for her to make. It was a choice between deciding whether to stay with me on terms that were far less hers than mine, or to leave me. "People always end up leaving me," she had told me on so many occasions. I wanted her to have a choice in the matter, without it being unilateral. She had professed to me many times that no one had ever loved her as much as I had loved her. Perhaps the fear of losing such love and commitment would shock her into realizing that she had to break away from the toxic routines and supports that she so relied on. There was enough good in her that if I could just have cut out the bad part, I would have been happy with what was left. But I also knew that she was who she was because of her whole, and that it was this complexity that had, in part, mystified and tantalized me.

I was disappointed that my love for her had not cured her, and that I would likely end up leaving her because of her inability to change. In my naiveté, I had been hurtful to her, building up her hope that this time would be different. And yet others had begun to see small positive changes in Jacqueline. She had been able to hold down a job for four months, longer and more consistently than ever before. Also, the times of crises were fewer, further between, and less intense. Her therapist asked her to invite me to the next session. The therapist told me that Jacqueline had made a breakthrough in recognizing just how much despair I must have felt at not seeing my family, but that she feared that my connection to them would destroy my love for her.

All of this was good, but it had been at the expense of my own sanity and emotional resources. If she couldn't by now internalize that I loved her, I was too empty to try any further.

CHAPTER 30

That Saturday was a day of apprehension. I knew that I was just hours away from taking a profoundly significant action, one that would change the course of my life forever, and my whole being sensed it. There were times in the preceding weeks when I had imagined this day, but was never brave enough to go through with it for fear that I would be seen as a failure. That was my greatest fear.

The senior resident gave me the rest of the day off work. When I arrived home I learned that Jacqueline was on an errand, so I used the opportunity to talk to her parents. I told them of my applications and interviews with residency programs. I let them know about the part-time job in England, and that my father had paid for a ticket to Europe and then on to America. They listened quietly. When I was done talking, Jacqueline's mother started to cry. "This is going to kill her. Aren't you worried that she will kill herself? Why did you marry her? You remember how you met her. You promised her." It was my turn to be silent, and then we were all quiet.

"I'm not exactly leaving her. I just don't want to live this way anymore. I want my own house. I want Jacqueline to have to face hard choices without having easy solutions. I appreciate all that you've done, but this

is not the life I wanted to live. This situation has not made her life any
better, and it has certainly made mine worse."

"Anthony, she'll never make it," she protested.

"If she can't make it then we'll never make it together. I can't give up my
dreams in order to spend the rest of my life taking care of her. Maybe I
made a serious mistake; I loved her then and I love her now, but I can't
give what I don't have left to give."

"You are leaving us to pick up the pieces."

"This is bigger than that. It is about my life too, not just hers. I'm dying
inside. At the end of the day you'll have to pick up the pieces anyway.
The only hope she has is if I'm strong enough to care for both of us. We
have to get out of this hopeless spiral."

"We have to start preparing her. Don't tell her about your plans yet."
They decided that they would let Jacqueline believe that they had lost
faith in me, thereby distancing themselves from me. She would have
them to turn to for support if she needed to.

After talking to them, I returned to our bedroom. I felt relaxed. More
than relaxed, I felt an odd peace thinking about how my life had taken
such a dramatic turn. With this peace came relief. Through the open
closet door, I saw one of my old belts hanging on a hook. I tried it on
and felt disgusted that it didn't reach around my waist. I threw it back in
the closet and then bent over to pick it up. I saw some torn papers lying
on the floor. I picked them up and recognized my now shredded, long-
lost surgery handbook. Jacqueline walked in. "Sorry," she laughed.
"Your damned job just made me so mad."

During the long days of the surgery rotation and during the tension-
filled moments that Jacqueline and I shared, I kept the certainty of my
leaving as a beacon of safety. When we bickered or fought, I nearly
blurted it out on each occasion. "You treat me like shit," I would say to
her in my thoughts, "That is why I have had it. I've gone behind your

back because you forced me to. I am leaving you because you don't let me breathe, because you don't share my dreams, because you are not my partner, because all you have ever cared about is yourself." But these were just thoughts that were driven by anger. I knew that she acted the way that she did because she was so afraid of being left alone. In order to be with me, she felt that she had to destroy anything that would get in the way of our being together, whether it was my love for my family or a simple textbook.

All her paranoia and fear forced me to think constantly of how every action that I made would make her feel, or how she would interpret it. I felt guilty that I was keeping a huge secret from her, and I felt that she would find out at any moment. The days were passing slowly, so I counted the hours, and then the minutes, and finally the seconds. "My parents have become really down on you these last few days. They told me that they don't think you'll be able to take care of me. I told them to fuck themselves. God, sometimes I can't stand them, especially my father. He's such a wimp. I never told you, but once a friend of mine got me a gun. My father had grounded me because I came in late one night. He made it into such a big issue. He lost his fucking mind. I thought that he was going to beat the crap out of me. Anyway, I sat in my room with the gun pointed at the door. If my father had walked in, I would have put a bullet in his head. He has no spine. He lets my mother walk all over him. He represents everything that I don't like in a man."

I wondered why she was telling me this story now. Had her parents told her about my earlier conversation with them? Was she threatening me? "Baby, you have taken better care of me than anybody ever did. I love you. I can't wait to get out of their house and find our own apartment." I felt affection towards her that I hadn't felt in some time for her having said that, but it was too little too late.

Six weeks to go. A Sunday in mid-November. I waited until after lunch to speak to her. We walked into the garden and I could see her parents through the dining room window pacing, looking back at us. She saw them too. "What's going on?"

"I got a job in England."

"What are you talking about?"

"Also, I have been offered some interviews in Boston for residency."

"When did all this happen?" She looked at her parents suspiciously.

"I'm doing this for us." I said quickly, defensively. I told her of my applications, and my early morning meetings with my father. I told her of the airplane ticket. I felt that I was back in my eighth grade Catholic-school confessional. She listened closely until I had stopped.

"You are such a liar. What you have done is worse than any slap in the face. It is worse than anything anybody has ever done to me. You go on with your plans, but I swear you'll regret it. You know that I'll never trust you again," she said calmly, then pleadingly added, "Anthony, why now? I was doing so well. Why?"

CHAPTER 31

The following Friday, I was assisting in an appendectomy when I got an urgent page to call home. The senior resident knew my situation. "Go ahead. I'll finish up here."

"Anthony." It was Jacqueline's mother. "She's done it again. She's taken a whole bunch of pills. We had to admit her to the hospital. Please come over as soon as you can."

"I'll be there as soon as possible." The resident gave me the day off, and I rushed to the hospital. Jacqueline was sharing a semi-private room with an older woman. I drew the separating curtain between them, and sat on Jacqueline's bed. Memories of a year earlier flooded back. I held her hand.

"I lied," she said. "I just took a couple of Tylenol. I wanted you to come back. I'm not going to make it without you. You say that you're drained, but you were able to put all those application packages together."

"That was self-preservation," I told her.

"Just thinking about you going makes me miss you already. We haven't been able to talk about it because you spend all your time at the hospital. I haven't had a chance to be with you." A naughty smile spread across her face. "I want to show you something," she said, leading me to the bathroom. Her roommate lifted a tired head off her pillow to look at us, then flopped back and closed her eyes. Jacqueline locked the door behind us, took my hand and slipped it between her legs. "Can you feel how much I've missed you? I've been wet since my mother told me that you were coming to the hospital. I want you right now. I want to know that you still love me." She dropped her soft white cotton robe to the floor. It had been months since we had been so uninhibited, but this time felt very different to me. Early in the relationship when we made love in the park or in the restaurant, it felt like it was part of the intensity that our relationship was built on and the intensity that would hold us together. Now I felt like a pretender, stealing a one-night stand knowing all the while that I was going to leave her, that she would not be able to make it with me outside of her safety net. For her though, the mood of the moment was what was real. "I feel so whole when we make love. I know that we can make it together. I've decided to go with you to England." We dressed hastily and left the bathroom. I felt guilty that her roommate "knew" and I almost apologized. Her visitors looked at us suspiciously. The next day Jacqueline was discharged from the hospital.

I returned to work, and the hours spent in the operating rooms were long. Jacqueline spent an occasional evening with me in the apartment in Pretoria, but we spent more time talking on the phone. Her mother called me frequently. Jacqueline seemed to be doing well, but her mother warned me that she was becoming more irritable. Jacqueline in turn told me that her mother was losing it.

Another Saturday morning arrived. I had just finished rounds with the resident when my pager went off. "Doctor Walker, please call home. It's an emergency." The resident gave me a kind, sympathetic look.
"Take all the time you need," he said. I phoned home, expecting to speak to Jacqueline's mother, but Jacqueline herself answered.
"It's my mother. She took an overdose of pills this morning. They took her to the hospital. God, she is such a child!"
"We're done with rounds," said the resident. "Go."

On the drive home, I wondered if her mother also had a personality disorder. Maybe she wasn't so disturbed that she couldn't function, but this overdose attempt seemed to me to be just as manipulative as anything that Jacqueline had ever done. I felt that she had done this to get back at me for threatening to leave Jacqueline. I wondered whether she thought that I would stay to take care of her, as I had taken care of Jacqueline just a year earlier. It felt like I had married not one, but two mentally ill women. "You are her guardian angel," her mother had told me. "Without you she would never have made it." I wasn't sure whether guardian angels were a big part of the Jewish faith, but they had been a cornerstone of our Catholic upbringing. Our angels would intercede for us to God and protect us from all evils, we were told. Maybe her mother using the term "guardian angel" had been a manipulation, appealing to my very early indoctrination. I saw manipulation in all of her actions, but I also understood why she did it. If she could not get somebody else to take care of her daughter, she would be the only one left to do it. Knowing her daughter, she had realized that she would never be able to do it alone.

Her mother looked tired and said that she was. When Jacqueline left the room to buy a box of chocolates, her mother sat up in bed. "It's so difficult to have her about the house without you being there. She takes so much. I can't do it on my own." The overdose had been minor but she took the time in the hospital to rest.

"She is so manipulative," complained Jacqueline.

I couldn't wait to get out of the madness.

CHAPTER 32

The final weeks passed calmly. Jacqueline seemed more withdrawn. "I don't know what I'm going to do. Just in case I don't make it with you, I've decided to start dating other men." She had always used this as a threat. Now it seemed like a realistic option. In a way I hoped that she could find somebody else. It would make my leaving easier.

Eventually, my internship came to a merciful end. I had a week off before my trip to England, and we spent the time together. Each day Jacqueline appeared sadder. She cried frequently and begged me to change my mind, but her rage did not show. Unable to say good-bye, she told me that she was going to take a vacation in Cape Town with her parents rather than come to the airport. With three days to go I had gone to my parents' house to pick up a suitcase for the trip. Jacqueline called me at my parents' home. "I've decided that this whole thing is just not going to work out. I have to look forward to my future, and I don't see that being with you. You know that I can get anyone I want. I met this guy at work the other day. He came to the counter. He's been coming to the counter a lot. He's got a lot of money. He asked me out. I have a date tonight."

"Fine."

"That's the way you want it? You're not going to stop me?"

"No, it's the way that you want it."

"If you don't want me to go, tell me now."

"It's your choice."

"I think I'll fuck him. He'll enjoy it. You know that."

"That's your choice too," I finished. She hung up. At seven that evening, she called me back.

"He's here. I just want you to keep the picture in your mind of him on top of me, inside me, kissing my breasts." She hung up again. At eight she was back on the phone. She was calling from the restaurant. "Babe, I'm having a terrible time. My stomach is hurting so much. I'm coming home now, please be there. You knew I would never do it. You have to know how much I'm going to miss you." The next day she left, miserably, with her parents. "Call me every day. Promise me that you will."

CHAPTER 33

Late December 1985
Jan Smuts International Airport

I waited nervously at the airport pacing back and forth in the lobby waiting for the ticket counter to open. I waited nervously at the check-in line, and then waited nervously at the gate. I waited nervously in my seat by the window. I was certain that she would do something to stop me. Maybe she would come running down the ramp yelling and screaming, begging for a last chance, acknowledging that she had made a terrible mistake. I waited for the captain to announce that they had been ordered by the tower to delay the departure. The gate closed and we taxied back a few feet then abruptly stopped. "Good evening ladies and gentlemen. We apologize for the abrupt stop but we have been ordered to stay in place…" I closed my eyes, "…as there is an emergency landing in the runway right in front of us. The delay will not be longer than twenty minutes." I breathed a little but counted the seconds slowly. Twenty minutes. "One Mississippi, two Mississippi, three Mississippi…" Twenty long Mississippi minutes went by, and then we moved. I melted back into my seat and closed my eyes as the thrust propelled the plane further away from my fears.

After a brief layover in New York, I finally touched down in Boston, and then, with residency interviews complete, I looked out back east across the Atlantic to Spain. I had not seen my Grandfather in some time. I needed a complete break before my part-time job in England was to begin.

Madrid was an eight hour flight, and yet a world away. Though the city air was polluted, it was the easiest I had breathed in a long time. The distance felt good. There was no threat of discovery, and I felt that I could do whatever I wanted to do. With every sip of sangria, the anxiety and tightness slowly washed away. At moments I felt guilty for feeling good, because it seemed that it was at Jacqueline's expense. It was precisely because she was not there that I could feel some peace. For what had felt to be an eternity, she had conditioned me not to feel any pleasure outside of her. Her fearsome tantrums had been intolerable in their wrath. Immediately I noticed that my sleep had improved. No longer did I worry that she might attack me in bed. My body felt more relaxed, my thoughts seemed slower and more focused. I felt that I could think about things without worrying about what Jacqueline would say or how she would react. But even with the distance from South Africa, I felt her presence and I jumped and startled when the phone rang or a car backfired.

The week in Spain refreshed me for the trip to England. The temporary job was in a North London hospital covering for the psychiatry service in the emergency room. Landing in gray Heathrow, the clouds seemed not so menacing and the air was the freshest yet. Jacqueline and I had agreed to talk on a weekly basis, after the daily schedule of phone-calls had become too complicated to coordinate. We had spent three weeks apart. One afternoon after a quenching pint in a pub in the Archway, I made my scheduled call. She sounded upbeat. "Sweetie, God, how I miss you. It's taken me all this time to see how good you are to me. I feel so empty without you. I realize that I can't go back to being without you. Everything has changed. I've treated you so badly. I've decided that

I am going to do it. We are going to make our life together. I'll be over next week." That evening, the house of emotional cards collapsed. I felt nervous and uncertain. No longer did I believe that I could cure her, but I knew that I had made her a promise; if she was willing to try to make the relationship work outside of South Africa, I too would try to make it work. If she was going to take the brave step of moving away from all that was familiar and certain to her, I felt that I could not abandon her. But what if she couldn't make it? We would be stuck in London with no one to turn to. Never had I felt so weak.

During the week, I resolved to be strong, to not allow her to damage the small gains in self-confidence that I had made in the short time we had been apart, to not allow myself to give in to her rage. She kept her promise to come, and I picked her up at Heathrow. The sight of her familiar smile reminded me of all the joy we had shared. Suddenly, I wondered whether my life with her had been as unpredictable and threatening as I remembered it to be. I realized how much I had missed her. Her face showed none of the torment and doubt that ravaged her mind. I waved at her and she started to cry, which made me cry. We rode a Black-Cab back to the apartment and made tea. It all seemed so normal. I wondered if the separation had made a significant impact on her. I prayed that the apparent change would be real.

Three days after her arrival, we were invited for dinner at the apartment of an old friend who had been slumming around England for the better part of a year. We drank a little too much wine and decided to walk back home rather than risk the perils of the Underground. "I see you had a good time tonight," said Jacqueline.
"I had fun. Didn't you?"
"Nothing's changed it seems. You still need other people to make you happy. I am not good enough for you." Immediately, I realized that my hopes that she had fundamentally changed, were false hopes. I recognized

the futility of our relationship. This realization struck me with the same certainty and clarity that I had experienced when I fell in love with her in the hospital only sixteen months earlier. I was overwhelmed with sadness. The relationship was dead. I was in love with a dream, but the morning had come and now I was wide awake. Jacqueline would never stay. Change would be too hard. Four weeks after she arrived in London, she returned, safely, to Johannesburg. She promised to come with me to Boston, but apart from on one other occasion, that was the last time I saw Jacqueline. After she left, both written correspondence and phone calls between us dwindled.

Boston University had accepted me into their psychiatry residency. I telephoned Jacqueline to let her know. "You need to know that I met a guy. He's fifty but he owns a Rolls Royce. He doesn't need to work so he can spend all his time with me. I don't love him, not like I loved you, but do you know what? Love is crap. It comes and it goes. I need someone who will take care of me." Her words stung as I replaced the receiver. The sense of failure would take a long time to deal with. I wondered about my own judgment. How would I ever be a good psychiatrist?

CHAPTER 34

June 1985
Boston

I arrived back in Boston with two suitcases and the money I had made in England. In three weeks the residency would start and I was glad to have the free time to settle in. I rented an apartment in the South End and ordered a mattress.

"We'll deliver next Friday between nine and one," promised the salesman. The apartment stood completely empty except for the refrigerator and the oven. I needed a bed before "next Friday." I went on a shopping expedition and found an army surplus store where I found a canvas stretcher. That would do until the mattress arrived. Boston was sticky. The Namibian desert had been hot, but I had never before felt such swelter. I carried the stretcher on my back and found a general store where I bought a spoon, knife and fork, a pot, a bowl and some canned foods. After a long walk back to the apartment, I took a tepid shower and set up the stretcher. I realized that I had nothing else to do. My mother had once warned me, "Only boring people get bored." I had never thought of myself as boring, but at that moment I didn't seem to have the energy to do anything.

That night I heated up some noodles, but they didn't appeal. I tried to read a book, but couldn't concentrate. I lay on the stretcher and realized just how alone I was. After more than a year of never being alone, I felt that I needed human contact like a drug addict needs his drug. I lay awake, unable to settle on the uncomfortable canvas. At three in the morning my thoughts were filled with doubt and misery,—doubt about my judgment and misery at the sense of having failed. I considered returning to Johannesburg and maybe back to Jacqueline, but I reminded myself how much I had to lose. Finally, the thought that I could surely never feel this low again brought some relief, and I fell asleep.

The next morning I awoke. I had a new sense of purpose. I needed to succeed. I wanted to do so on my own, even though I felt exhausted after my year with Jacqueline. I could barely wait for the residency to begin, and when it did, I worked harder than I had ever worked. Slowly the tide of depression began to turn. I had started to smoke but soon stopped. I ate healthier and ran a mile every day. I tested the waters of new friendships, quickly withdrawing at the merest hint of neediness. I was mistrustful of kindness, confusing it for manipulation. A year of hard work, though, made the year fly by. I began to laugh at myself, to trust my feelings and judgment. I was better able to relax, to drink wine for its own pleasure rather than to escape.

One evening, soon after I had moved into a new apartment in Brighton, Jacqueline surprised me with a call. I had not given her my number. She told me that my father had given it to her. "I told him that I wanted to talk to you about a divorce. He gave me your number in a heartbeat."
"How are you doing?" I felt strangely comforted by her voice.
"I was thinking of coming out to Boston to visit you. Just for two weeks. I promise. I feel that I treated you so badly during the time we were together. I just want to say that I'm sorry. I want to be your friend. I don't have to stay with you. You could find me a hotel room." I wanted

to believe that she had changed. I wanted this for me, but I wanted it for her even more. I still felt affection and care for her, but I knew that my wish for her to be better could not make it so.

"Sorry, Jacqueline, we've been through too much for the visit to be good for either of us. It's so easy to forget all the stuff that didn't work out. We remember the good times because they bought us such joy. The other stuff drove us apart. Never underestimate the power of denial to erase the hurt that lies between us." She was silent for a minute.

"I'll speak to you soon."

We spoke twice more by phone and then the phone calls ended.

The issue of our marriage remained. I was not with her and could not remain married to her. I was beginning to feel whole again. I had to close the book on this chapter in my life. I called my father and asked him to help me find a divorce lawyer. My father arranged it quickly, and two years after moving to Boston, I flew back to Johannesburg.

The day after I landed, I had to present myself in court. I wondered whether Jacqueline would appear. I worried that she would contest the divorce. I turned each time someone entered the court to see if it was her, but she did not show up, and as quick as our wedding ceremony had been, so were the divorce proceedings. Both had lasted five minutes.

POSTSCRIPT

On my first day of legal freedom, my mother and I went for a walk to a new shopping center in town. Halfway there, we turned in response to the screeching of car-tires behind us. It was Jacqueline. She peered out of the driver's window, and then smiled. "My God, look who's back! Where are you going?"

"Hi! We're off to the mall," I told her.

"Jump in, I'll give you a ride." My mother hesitated for a second, then agreed. We arrived at the mall a few minutes later, and I sent my mother off. "We have some last unfinished business, Mom."

"OK, I'll meet you inside in twenty minutes."

"They still want to protect you from me," said Jacqueline, smiling but without malice. "I don't know how you ever put up with me. I treated you so badly." She looked beautiful and relaxed.

"I treated you badly too. I promised you something I could not do. To stay with you forever."

"You and all the other men," she said wistfully. "Hey, why don't we go out for dinner tonight, just for old time's sake? I'm sure you're going back to Boston soon. A meal, a drink and then home. I promise. OK, maybe sex too, but we're divorced, so there is no commitment." She laughed. I looked at her and smiled. I remembered the day I had met her, and how, even with the tubes and the intravenous lines, she had seduced me. I thought about how quickly I had fallen for her. I wondered briefly if a dinner would be so dangerous, but then the memory of the rest of the relationship quickly returned.

"I'm glad you stopped. We hadn't had a chance to say good-bye. I don't think that dinner would be a good idea."

"OK. Think about it. Here's my number. Call me if you want." She leaned across and kissed my cheek. That was the last time I ever saw or heard from her again.

In the mall, my mother had waited the twenty, and then thirty minutes. She came out to look for me. By chance, an ambulance had arrived in response to an unrelated emergency. I saw my mother come running out of the mall. "Mom, where are you going?" I shouted after her. She turned in disbelief.

"I saw the ambulance. I thought that she had done something to you. What took you so long?"

"We were married for a year. We had to say good-bye."

The dance was over.

A FINAL NOTE

Because I work in the field of psychiatry, I have had many opportunities to work with Borderline Personality sufferers and their families. During these times, I have seen interactions and relationships that reminded me of my relationship with Jacqueline and her family. I believe that my relationship with Jacqueline strengthened my understanding of others' suffering, and because of this, has made me a better therapist.

My relationship with Jacqueline further taught me a lot about the way that I think. It taught me to continuously monitor my thoughts and feelings, especially when I work with Borderline sufferers. I feel that I understand Borderline Personality disorder in my bones. Many old memories, and some anxieties, are rekindled when I meet and work with Borderline patients. I cannot feel their sense of desperation and numbness, but I understand how terrible their existence can be. I also know how tremendously draining their illness can be for those who love them.

It is true that the life of the person suffering from Borderline Personality is dictated and directed by the disorder. It is further true that to some extent, the lives of those sharing the sufferer's life are dictated and directed by the disorder. By its very nature, it is a life of extremes.

Extremes of anger and love, sadness and joy, hope and despair, and sometimes even life and death. The disorder can ultimately lead to suicide. It is so intolerable that the sufferer sometimes chooses death over the pain of the living with the condition. When the behavior is so often driven by desperation, it is easy to forget that the behavior is not a choice. It is so much easier to be frustrated and angry, and to blame the sufferer.

Treatment does require love, and more than love, compassion. The love that is needed is not a romantic love, but a desire to care. It is easy to confuse the two because of the Borderline sufferer's seductive neediness. It is a neediness that appeals to our desire to help. The error is to love without limits or consistency. The error is to be alone in caring for the sufferer. The error is to believe that love alone will do it.

Hope lies in time. Healing comes when the Borderline patient eventually internalizes both trust in others, and a stable sense of self. These are developmental processes, which take time to mature. The change can come, although slowly, and in the care of compassionate and patient hands.

Living with anybody who suffers from a chronic illness can be emotionally taxing. Moreover, living with someone who has a chronic mental illness means at times having to accept erratic behavior, unpredictability, and loss of autonomy. No amount of intellectualization and rationalization about the illness can ever truly remove the sometimes-ruinous effects on the relationship. In my case my instinct for self-preservation told me that I could no longer continue to be with Jacqueline and have a fulfilling life. It is frequently not the case, however, that the effects of a condition are so destructive to a relationship.

Appendix I

Diagnostic criteria for 301.83
Borderline Personality Disorder

A pervasive pattern of instability of interpersonal relationships, self-image, and affects, and marked impulsivity beginning by early adulthood and present in a variety of contexts, as indicated by five (or more) of the following:

1. frantic efforts to avoid real or imagined abandonment. **Note:** Do not include suicidal or self-mutilating behavior covered in Criterion 5.
2. a pattern of unstable and intense interpersonal relationships characterized by alternating between extremes of idealization and devaluation
3. identity disturbance: markedly and persistently unstable self-image or sense of self
4. impulsivity in at least two areas that are potentially self-damaging (e.g., spending, sex, substance abuse, reckless driving, binge eating). **Note:** Do not include suicidal or self-mutilating behavior covered in Criterion 5.
5. recurrent suicidal behavior, gestures, or threats, or self-mutilating behavior

6. affective instability due to a marked reactivity of mood (e.g., intense episodic dysphoria, irritability, or anxiety usually lasting a few hours and only rarely more than a few days)
7. chronic feelings of emptiness
8. inappropriate, intense anger or difficulty controlling anger (e.g., frequent displays of temper, constant anger, recurrent physical fights)
9. transient, stress-related paranoid ideation or severe dissociative symptoms

Familial Pattern

Borderline Personality Disorder is about five times more common among first-degree biological relatives of those with the disorder than in the general population. There is also an increased familial risk for Substance-Related Disorders, Antisocial Personality Disorder, and Mood Disorders.

Specific Culture, Age, and Gender Features

The pattern of behavior seen in Borderline Personality Disorder has been identified in many settings around the world. Adolescents and young adults with identity problems (especially when accompanied by substance use) may transiently display behaviors that misleadingly give the impression of Borderline Personality Disorder. Such situations are characterized by emotional instability, "existential" dilemmas, uncertainty, anxiety-provoking choices, conflicts about sexual orientation, and competing social pressures to decide on careers. Borderline Personality Disorder is diagnosed predominantly (about 75%) in females.

Prevalence

The prevalence of Borderline Personality Disorder is estimated to be about 2% of the general population, about 10% among individuals seen in outpatient mental health clinics, and about 20% among psychiatric inpatients. It ranges from 30% to 60% among clinical populations with Personality Disorders.

Course

There is considerable variability in the course of Borderline Personality Disorder. The most common pattern is one of chronic instability in early adulthood, with episodes of serious affective and impulsive dyscontrol and high levels of use of health and mental health resources. The impairment from the disorder and the risk of suicide are greatest in the young-adult years and gradually wane with advancing age. During their 30s and 40s, the majority of individuals with this disorder attain greater stability in their relationships and vocational functioning.

Printed in the United States
2665